COVENTRY CITY FC

An A–Z

Dean Hayes

S.B. Publications

DEDICATION

To Sky Blues' fans everywhere

First published in 2000 by S. B. Publications,
c/o 19 Grove Road, Seaford, East Sussex BN25 1TP

ISBN 1 85770 201 8

Designed and typeset by CGB, Lewes
Printed by MFP Design & Print
Longford Trading Estate, Thomas Street
Stretford, Manchester M32 0JT

ACKNOWLEDGEMENTS

The author would like to express his thanks to the following organisations for their help:
Coventry City Football Club, The Association of Football Statisticians, The Football League; British Newspaper Library; Coventry Record Library, The Harris Library, Preston.
Thanks also to the following individuals: Ben Hayes, David Higson, Iain Price and Stephen Whittle.

PICTURE CREDITS

Illustrations were kindly supplied by the *Lancashire Evening Post* – with others from the author's own collection.

Front cover: Top left: Willie Carr, bottom left: Jeff Blockley.
Centre: Steve Ogrizovic. Top right: Brian Borrows,
bottom right: Brian Kilcline.

ABOUT THE AUTHOR

Dean Hayes is an experienced freelance sports writer specialising in football and cricket. He was educated at Hayward Grammar School, Bolton and West Midlands College of Physical Education and was a Primary School Head Teacher until taking up writing on a permanent basis four years ago.

He has played football in the Lancashire Amateur League, but he now concentrates solely on playing the summer game.

This former cricket professional, now playing as an amateur, has taken well over 2,000 wickets in league cricket.

Dean is married to Elaine and has one son and two stepchildren. This is his forty first football book to be published and his fifty second overall.

INTRODUCTION

Coventry City Football Club was formed in 1883 by workers at Singer's bicycle factory and first played under the title Singer's FC. It acquired its current name in 1898 and a year later moved into the Highfield Road ground.

Coventry finally joined the Football League in 1919, as members of the Second Division, and subsequently divided their time between the Second and Third Divisions, except for 1958–59 when they spent one season in the Fourth Division. In 1967 they established themselves as long-term members of the First Division and have since spent the last thirty three seasons in the top flight.

The 1960s were a time of great change and controversy for Coventry City Football Club and the period is still referred to as the 'Sky Blue era'. Manager Jimmy Hill under the chairmanship of Derrick Robbins completely revitalised the entire image of the club. Not only did the team play in a more striking sky blue strip but there were Sky Blue trains for travelling fans and Sky Blue radio to entertain the supporters before matches.

The team soon began to prosper and in 1987 the climax arrived when John Sillett's side won the FA Cup after beating Tottenham Hotspur 3–2 in the Final.

Dean Hayes
August 2000

ABANDONED MATCHES

An abandoned match may be defined as one which is called off by the referee while it is in progress because conditions do not permit it to be completed. Far fewer matches are abandoned in modern times because if there is some doubt about the ability to play the full game, the match is more likely to be postponed.

Below is a full list of abandoned matches involving Coventry City.

Date	Opponents	Competition	Score	Reason
28.11.1903 ·	Halesowen (H)	Birmingham Lg	3–1	Fog (82 mins)
02.12.1905	Stafford R (H)	Birmingham Lg	1–1	Rain (60 mins)
19.10.1907	Bilston (A)	FA Cup	2–1	Hailstorm (70 mins)
06.03.1909	Reading (A)	Southern Lg	0–1	Rain (45 mins)
01.10.1910	Northampton (A)	Southern Lg	0–0	Bad light (51 mins)
04.12.1937	Southampton (H)	Division 2	1–0	Snow (45 mins)
19.11.1949	Sheff Wed (H)	Division 2	1–0	Fog (63 mins)
26.03.1955	Southend.U (H)	Division 3(S)	3–1	Rain (68 mins)
22.12.1956	Crystal P (H)	Division 3(S)	0–0	Floodlight failure (51 mins)
25.12.1956	Newport C (A)	Division 3(S)	0–0	Blizzard (71 mins)
22.12.1962	Colchester U (H)	Division 3	2–0	Fog (45 mins)
04.03.1972	Sheff Utd (H)	Division 1	0–2	Rain(62 mins)
25.11.1972	Ipswich T (A)	Division 1	1–0	Floodlight failure (61 mins)

AGGREGATE SCORE

Coventry City's highest aggregate score in any competition came in the Football League Cup of 1985–86. When playing Chester City the Sky Blues notched up nine goals over the two legs. They won the first leg at Sealand Road 2–1 and then 7–2 at Highfield Road with Cyrille Regis scoring five of the goals to win 9–3 on aggregate.

ALLEN, TOMMY

Goalkeeper Tommy Allen joined Southampton on a free transfer from Sunderland in May 1920. In 1921–22 he was ever-present as the Saints won the Third Division (South) Championship and kept twenty six clean sheets in forty two games – still a club record. He went on to play in 323 League and Cup games, notching up a record 291 league appearances for a Southampton goalkeeper before leaving The Dell in the close season of 1928 to play for Coventry.

He made his league debut in a 3–0 home win over Norwich City on the opening day of the 1928–29 season. He was ever–present in that campaign and again the following season, going on to play in 103 consecutive League and Cup games from his debut. Nicknamed 'Shadow', Allen appeared in 164 games during his four seasons at Highfield Road before playing for Accrington Stanley and Northampton Town.

APPEARANCES

The players with the highest number of appearances for Coventry City are as follows:

		League	FA Cup	Lg Cup	Others	Total
1	Steve Ogrizovic	504	34	49	11	598
2	George Curtis	483 (4)	29	22	–	534 (4)
3	Mick Coop	413 (12)	25 (1)	36(1)	11	485 (14)
4	Brian Borrows	396 (13)	26	42	10(1)	474 (14)
5	Bill Glazier	346	21	25	10	402
6	Mick Kearns	344	24	14	–	382
7	Tommy Hutchison	312 (2)	23	18	–	353(2)
8	George Mason	330	20	–	–	350
9	Roy Kirk	330	15	–	–	345
10	Trevor Peake	277(1)	17	30	10	334(1)

ATKINSON, RON

Unable to make the grade at Villa Park, Ron Atkinson was given a free transfer and joined Headington United in 1959. They changed their name to Oxford United the following year and Atkinson, converted to wing-half, captained the side to great success. They won the Southern League

Championship in both the 1960–61 and 1961–62 seasons and replaced the defunct Accrington Stanley in the Football League. Atkinson served Oxford for fifteen years, playing in 560 matches, 383 of them in the Football League. He helped them win promotion from the Fourth Division in 1965 and climb into the Second Division three years later.

He began his managerial career at Kettering Town and in his first season took them to the Southern League North Division Championship and promotion to the Premier League. He then joined Cambridge United and led them to the Fourth Division Championship. They were on course for a second successive promotion when he joined West Bromwich Albion.

After the Baggies had finished third in Division One in 1979–80 Atkinson moved to Manchester United. The Old Trafford side won the FA Cup in 1983 and 1985 but in 1986 Big Ron was sacked, receiving

Ron Atkinson.

£100,000 in compensation. After a short second spell at the Hawthorns he was enticed to join Atletico Madrid but after just 86 days, he was sacked. In February 1989 he became manager of Sheffield Wednesday and despite suffering relegation in 1989–90, returned to the top flight the following season and won the League Cup. In the summer of 1991 Atkinson joined Aston Villa and in 1992–93 led them to the runners-up spot in the Premier League. Villa also won the League Cup but in October 1994, after a run of eight defeats and a draw in nine matches, he was sacked.

In February 1995 he took over at Coventry City and after winning his first game in charge 2–0 against West Ham United, went on to win the Manager of the Month award for March, as the club was undefeated in his first six matches. In each of Atkinson's two seasons at Highfield Road, the club finished sixteenth in the Premier League. In 1996–97 both Atkinson and his assistant, Gordon Strachan, were in trouble with the FA on disrepute charges. Big Ron's plans to promote Strachan to manager came about in November 1996 after he had moved 'upstairs'.

7

In 1998–99 he took over the reins of Nottingham Forest but after failing to keep the Reds in the Premier League, he left the City Ground club.

ATTENDANCE – AVERAGE

The average home league attendance for Coventry City over the last ten seasons has been as follows:

1990–91	13,794	1995–96	18,507
1991–92	13,876	1996–97	19,625
1992–93	14,951	1997–98	19,718
1993–94	13,352	1998–99	20,778
1994–95	15,980	1999–00	20,828

ATTENDANCE – HIGHEST

The record attendance at Highfield Road is 51,455 for the Second Division game with Wolverhampton Wanderers on 29 April 1967. The Sky Blues who won 3–1 with goals from Machin, Gibson and Rees went on to win the Second Division Championship, being undefeated in their last twenty five league matches.

ATTENDANCE – LOWEST

The lowest attendance at Highfield Road was 1,086 for the visit of Millwall on 15 October 1985 for a Full Members' Cup tie. The match ended 1–1 with Terry Gibson scoring for the Sky Blues.

AUSTIN, FRANK

An England Schoolboy international, Frank Austin joined the Sky Blues from Toton FC in 1950 and made his debut at left-back in a 1–0 home defeat by Newport County in April 1953. He appeared in one other game towards the end of that season before establishing himself as a regular first team member in 1953–54. Over the next nine seasons Austin missed very few games but in 1956 was converted to full-back. Here his strong tackling and good distributional skills were put to better use and in 1958–59 he helped the club win promotion to the Third Division.

Austin was at Highfield Road for thirteen years, during which time he had played under seven managers. Jimmy Hill was manager in 1963 who allowed him to join Torquay United after appearing in 313 League and Cup games for Coventry. He played in twenty four league games for the Plainmoor club before leaving the first class scene.

AWAY MATCHES

Coventry City's best away win is the 7–0 defeat of Aberdare Athletic on 18 April 1927. They also scored seven goals away from home on 30 December 1933 when they won 7–3 at Gillingham. The club's worst defeat away from home is 10–2 by Norwich City on 15 March 1930.

AWAY SEASONS

The club's highest number of away wins came in 1969–70 when it won ten of its twenty one matches in finishing sixth in the First Division. Coventry's fewest away wins (one) occurred in seasons 1924–25, 1931–32, 1967–68 and 1990–91.

B

BARRATT, HARRY

The son of Southampton forward Josiah Barratt, he joined City in 1935 but did not make his league debut until April 1938 when he starred in the club's 3–2 home win over Blackburn Rovers. This followed a loan spell at Cheltenham Town and a series of impressive performances for the Reserves. Though he only made four appearances in 1938–39, the last season of League football before the war, he made 112 appearances for City during the hostilities, scoring forty four goals including four in a match on three occasions – Notts County (Home 8–2 in 1943–44) Newport County (Home 7–1 in 1945–46) and Millwall (Home 7–2 in 1945–46).

When League football resumed in 1946–47 Barratt was a virtual ever-present for the next five seasons and in the last four of those, was captain. He was a most versatile player, wearing seven different numbered out-field shirts and even had a spell in goal when Alf Wood was injured. He played the last of his 178 League and Cup games for the club on the opening day of the 1951–52 season when he was injured and forced to retire. After a spell managing Rugby Town he was appointed Coventry's chief scout but left shortly after Jesse Carver's departure to manage Gillingham.

BAYLISS, DICK

Following an unspectacular playing career with Luton Town, Mansfield and Southend United, Dick Bayliss became Harry Storer's chief scout and coach in 1931 and was the obvious choice to take over from him at Highfield Road when Storer left for Birmingham City.

Bayliss was an excellent judge of a player and brought many talented footballers to Coventry before the Second World War. He was appointed

Coventry City manager in June 1945 and, after the transistional season of 1945–46, Bayliss and his team were ready for the resumption of League football.

Coventry were a talented but ageing side and were soon struggling. Sadly, Bayliss' health began to deteriorate and he became ill after a nightmare drive back from Southend during the big freeze of 1947. Soon afterwards he died of kidney failure at the early age of forty seven. Bayliss who had been extremely popular with all the players, never really had the time to develop his own team.

BENNETT, DAVE

Winger Dave Bennett started his Football League career with Manchester City. He had scored nine goals in fifty two league games and appeared in the 1981 FA Cup Final replay against Tottenham Hotspur when Cardiff City paid £120,000 to take him to Ninian Park.

Playing in the same Bluebirds' side as his brother Gary, he helped the Welsh club win promotion to the Second Division in 1982–83 when he scored twelve goals in forty league games. After failing to reach agreement over terms Bennett, who had scored twenty goals in eighty nine games, joined Coventry City for £120,000, a figure fixed by an independent tribunal.

He played his first game for the Sky Blues in a 2–1 home win over Leicester City in September 1983, going on to be a first team regular at Highfield Road for five seasons. In 1987 he won an FA Cup winners' medal as Coventry beat Spurs 3–2. Bennett scored one and made another of the goals as the Sky Blues won their first major honour.

On leaving Highfield Road, Bennett who had scored thirty three goals in 208 games, played for Sheffield Wednesday, for Swindon Town and for Shrewsbury Town before leaving the league scene.

Dave Bennett.

BEST, JERRY

Goalkeeper Jerry Best made his Coventry debut against Cardiff City at Highfield Road on Christmas Day 1920. The Welsh club were pressing for promotion to the First Division and beat the Sky Blues 4–2. Best kept his place for the return game at Ninian Park two days later and turned in a magnificent performance in a surprise 1–0 win for the visitors. After that he was a virtual fixture in the Coventry side and was ever-present in the seasons of 1922–23, 1923–24 and 1924–25, appearing in 170 consecutive league games during that run.

In November 1925 he became the club's first League player to be awarded a testimonial but at the end of the 1925–26 season he was sold to Halifax Town in an exchange deal which brought Jack Newton to Highfield Road. At the time of his departure, his total of 236 League and Cup appearances was a club record.

His stay at The Shay was brief and he soon moved to Rotherham where he ended his league career, later playing non-league football for Worksop Town.

BEST STARTS

Coventry City were unbeaten for the first fifteen matches of the 1937–38 Second Division campaign in which they finished fourth, winning seven and drawing eight of their matches. Their first defeat came at home to Sheffield Wednesday on 20 November 1937 when they went down 1–0.

BIRMINGHAM LEAGUE

Singers FC joined the Birmingham League in 1894, playing matches against the reserve sides of Aston Villa, Small Heath, West Bromwich Albion and Wolverhampton Wanderers. Because the club was unable to hold on to its star players, it struggled in its first few seasons in the competition. In 1894–95 the side suffered 8–0 defeats at the hands of West Bromwich Albion and Wolverhampton Wanderers reserves and again at the Molineux club the following season. In 1897–98, Singers lost 11–3 at Bristol Eastville Rovers and two seasons later lost 7–6 against the same opposition. The club's heaviest defeat in the Birmingham League came in

1900–01 when they lost 14–1 to Aston Villa reserves. Their biggest win, 11–2 against West Bromwich Albion reserves, came in the very last match they played in the Birmingham League on 29 April 1908, a season in which they finished fourth.

BLOCKLEY, JEFF

Jeff Blockley was captain of Coventry City's youth team when they reached the FA Youth Cup Final of 1968 and the following season made his first team debut as a substitute in a 1–0 defeat at Southampton. It was 1969–70 when Blockley became a regular member of the Sky Blues'

side, missing very few games over the next four seasons. He was ever-present in 1970–71 and 1971–72 during the course of which he took his total of consecutive league appearances to 108. His performances at the heart of the Coventry defence led to him winning six England Under-23 caps and selection for the Football League. He had scored ten goals in 167 League and Cup games for City when he was transferred to Arsenal for £200,000 in October 1972. Seven days after putting pen to paper he made his only full international appearance for England in a 1–1 draw against Yugoslavia at Wembley.

Blockley's time at Highbury was not a happy one and in January 1975, after appearing in sixty two games for the Gunners, he was

Jeff Blockley.

allowed to leave and join his home club, Leicester City, for £100,000. He made seventy five appearances for the Foxes before following a loan spell

Jim Blyth in action for Scotland.

with Derby County, he moved to Notts County where he ended his league career. He later played non-league football for Gloucester City before managing Leicester United.

BLYTH, JIM

Goalkeeper Jim Blyth was on Preston North End's books when Coventry paid £20,000 for his services in October 1972. The Highfield Road club also had to pay an extra £10,000 when Blyth played in the Sky Blues' first team and won international honours for Scotland. Blyth's first team debut was three years in coming as he understudied first Bill Glazier and then Bryan King. He eventually played his first game in the senior side in December 1975 as City lost 2–1 at home to Everton. He then appeared in fifty consecutive league games for the Sky Blues before damaging a knee in a 1–1 draw at home to West Ham United in April 1977.

He returned to first team action the following season and helped the club to finish in seventh place in the First Division. His consistent displays earned him a call up to the Scotland side and he made his full international debut against Bulgaria. On his second appearance for Scotland Blyth was involved in a misunderstanding with Willie Donachie which led to the full-back putting through his own goal. Sadly, this incident probably cost the Perth-born 'keeper his place in Scotland's World Cup squad.

Over the next four seasons, Blyth shared the goalkeeping duties with Les Sealey but after appearing in 174 League and Cup games for the Sky Blues, he left to join Birmingham City on a free transfer. At St Andrew's he found himself understudying both Tony Coton and David Seaman and after three years with the club left to play non-league football for Nuneaton Borough.

BORROWS, BRIAN

Brian Borrows started his career with his local club, Everton, making his Football League debut against Stoke City at Goodison Park in February 1982. However, he was unable to establish a regular first team place and was allowed to join Bolton Wanderers for £10,000 in March 1983. The Lancashire club were struggling at the foot of the Second Division and despite Borrows' fine performances at right-back, they were relegated to the Third Division. It was obvious that he was too good a player for this

Brian Borrows.

standard of football and in the summer of 1985, after appearing in 110 games for the Wanderers, he joined Coventry City for a fee of £80,000.

He made his Sky Blues debut in a 1–1 draw at home to Manchester City on the opening day of the 1985–86 season and went on to play in all but one of that campaign's league games. He was unlucky to lose the opportunity of an FA Cup winners' medal in 1987, when an injury sustained in the last league game of the season against Southampton ruled him out of the final against Spurs.

He has since had the consolation of being voted the Highfield Road club's Player of the Year in 1990 when he won his only international honour, a 'B' cap against Czechoslovakia.

Borrows was a model of consistency during his twelve seasons at Highfield Road, scoring thirteen goals in 488 League and Cup games.

He had a loan spell with Bristol City in September 1993, then joined Swindon Town on loan. After a number of impressive performances he was signed on a free transfer.

BOURTON, CLARRIE

Bristol-born Clarrie Bourton played his early football for Paulton United while working as a printer. He joined Bristol City in the close season of 1927 but after only four first team games he left to join Blackburn Rovers in a deal which also took Albert Keating to Ewood Park and brought a fee of £3,650 to Ashton Gate. He scored thirty seven goals in sixty eight games for the Lancashire club before Harry Storer paid £750 to bring him to Highfield Road in the summer of 1931.

He made his debut for Coventry in a 5–3 defeat at Fulham on the opening day of the 1931–32 season. Although he failed to score in that game, he ended the season as the Football League's top goalscorer with forty nine goals in forty games. Bourton, who scored in a club record ten successive games, netted five goals in a 6–1 home win over Bournemouth, four goals in a 5–1 defeat of Mansfield Town and hat-tricks against Clapton Orient (Home 4–2) Reading (Home 5–1) Crystal Palace (Home 8–0) Mansfield Town (Away 3–3) and Watford (Home 5–0).

In 1932–33 he scored forty goals in thirty nine league games and was second in the Football League charts to Hull City's Bill McNaughton. He scored in nine consecutive league games but only netted one hat-trick in the 6–0 home win over former club Bristol City. Forming a good understanding with Jock Lauderdale, he continued to score goals for City and in 1933–34, his total of twenty five included four goals in the 9–0 demolition of Bristol City and hat-tricks against Swindon Town (Home 5–1) and Torquay United (Away 3–1). He scored twenty six goals in thirty nine league games the following season and in 1935–36, when the club won the Third Division (South) Championship, his total of twenty four goals included hat-tricks in the wins over Newport County (Home 7–1) and Crystal Palace (Home 8–1).

In six seasons at Highfield Road, Bourton scored 180 goals in 241 League and Cup games before leaving to play for Plymouth Argyle in October 1937. He was unable to settle at Home Park and returned to play for Bristol City where in 1938–39 he was appointed caretaker-manager after Bob Hewison had been suspended by the FA for making illegal payments to amateurs. Before retiring in 1944 he saw the Ashton Gate club into a respectable position in the top half of the table before reverting to a non-managerial position when Hewison's suspension was lifted.

BROTHERS

Garry and Keith Thompson both played for Coventry City. Garry Thompson joined the club as an apprentice and during his six seasons in the first team scored forty nine goals in 158 League and Cup games. He won six England Under-21 caps during his time at Highfield Road before later playing for West Bromwich Albion, Aston Villa, Watford and Crystal Palace.

Keith Thompson appeared in thirty games for the Sky Blues in two spells after leaving to play for Real Oviedo. His only goal for the club came in a 1–1 home draw against West Ham United on 5 November 1988.

BROWN, EDDIE

Former theological student Eddie Brown, who had studied in the Channel Islands before being evacuated during the war, was one of the game's fastest strikers. He started his career with Preston North End where he scored fourteen goals in thirty one league games before moving to Southampton in September 1950 in a part exchange deal which saw Charlie Wayman go in the opposite direction.

One of the game's great characters, he ended his first season at The Dell as the club's top scorer with twenty goals in thirty six appearances. He started the following campaign in a similar vein and had scored twelve goals in twenty one games including a hat-trick in a 5–2 win over Nottingham Forest when he asked for a transfer.

He moved to Coventry City and made his debut at the City Ground but this time Forest ran out winners 3–1. He scored three goals in the last nine games of the season but could not prevent Coventry from being relegated. In 1952–53 he was the club's leading scorer with nineteen goals and topped the charts again the following season with twenty goals in thirty three games including a hat-trick in a 3–0 win at Colchester United. He had scored nine goals in the opening twelve games of the 1954–55 season, including another hat-trick in a 3–2 win at Brentford, when he was sold to Birmingham City.

Brown, who had scored fifty one goals in eighty nine games for the Highfield Road club, appeared in Birmingham's FA Cup Final side of 1956. He later played for Leyton Orient, taking his total of goals scored to 190 in 399 league appearances for his five clubs.

BROWN, JACKIE

Having played his early football with Belfast Celtic, Jackie Brown was signed for Wolverhampton Wanderers by Major Buckley in 1934. At Molineux he faced stiff competition for the wing positions with George Ashall and in two seasons with the club only appeared in twenty seven eague games.

During the early part of the 1936–37 season Coventry's McNestry damaged an ankle in a 2–0 win over Plymouth Argyle so manager Harry Storer acted quickly and signed Brown for £3,000.

He was already an Irish international when he arrived at Highfield Road and in his two seasons with the club, added to his collection by representing both Northern Ireland and the Republic of Ireland.

He made his debut in a 4–0 home win over West Ham United and went on to end the season as the club's leading scorer with thirteen goals in twenty nine league games. He topped the club's scoring charts again in 1937–38, netting another thirteen goals from forty league games. All told, Brown scored twenty nine goals in seventy three League and Cup games before the signing of George Ashall prompted his departure to Birmingham for £3,000.

He was a regular in the St Andrew's club side in 1938–39 and played in a few wartime games. After the hostilities he turned out for Barry Town and Bristol Rovers before joining Ipswich Town where he ended his league career.

BRUCK, DIETMAR

Dietmar Bruck made his Coventry City debut at the age of seventeen years nine days in a 1–1 draw at home to Swindon Town on the final day of the 1960–61 season. Although he played in a handful of games the following season it was 1962–63 before he established himself as a first team regular. During that season he scored in the FA Cup fifth round win over Sunderland and opened his league account in the 5–4 win over Halifax Town. However, despite his performances during that campaign he was forced to share the wing–half duties over the next few seasons with Farmer and Hill and in 1963–64 when the club won the Third Division Championship he only made ten appearances.

When Allan Harris left to join Chelsea, Bruck moved to left-back and in 1966–67 won a Second Division Championship medal as the club entered the top flight for the first time in their history. Again he began to face stiff competition from new signing Chris Cattlin and, after moving to right-back, from Mick Coop and Wilf Smith.

He had scored eight goals in 217 games when he left Highfield Road to play for Charlton Athletic. He later ended his league career with Northampton Town before becoming player/manager of Weymouth Town. After hanging up his boots he managed a number of non-league clubs in the Midlands.

BUCKLE, HARRY

Irish international Harry Buckle had played for Sunderland and Bristol Rovers when he joined Coventry just before the start of the 1908–09 season. He made his debut in a 1–1 draw at home to Crystal Palace on the opening day of the club's Southern League campaign. Missing just one game, he was the Sky Blue's top scorer with seventeen goals including a hat-trick in a 5–3 home win over Portsmouth. Just before the start of the following season Buckle, who was highly thought of by the club's directors, was appointed team manager.

His response was to top the club's charts again with seventeen goals and to see his side move up twelve places in the Southern League. He continued to find the net in the 1910–11 season and netted another hat-trick for the club in a 5–1 home win over Southend United.

Buckle, who had scored forty six goals in 125 games, left the club at the end of that campaign to join Belfast Celtic. Surprisingly he was still playing football after the First World War and won Cup medals in 1924 and 1926 when playing for Fordsons, Ford League of Ireland team based in Cork..

BUTCHER, TERRY

Terry Butcher was born in Singapore where his father was in the Royal Navy. This competitive and commanding central defender began his Football League career with Ipswich Town, establishing himself as a first team regular in 1978–79. In 1980, Butcher won his first full cap for England when he played against Australia after winning honours at Under 21 and 'B' international level. Later that season he helped Ipswich to a UEFA Cup Final victory over AZ67 Alkmaar and to runners-up in the First Division. Butcher who was Player of the Year in 1984–85 became captain but in 1986 after the Portman Road club had been relegated, he left to join Glasgow Rangers for £725,000.

At Ibrox Park he won three Scottish Premier League Championship medals, three Scottish League Cup winners' medals and a Scottish Cup runners–up medal.

Butcher, who won seventy seven caps for his country, played in three

World Cup finals including skippering England to the semi–finals in 1990.

He fell out with Rangers' manager Graeme Souness and in November 1990 joined Coventry City as player/manager. He made his debut in a 1–0 home defeat by Liverpool in a first season which saw the Sky Blues struggle against relegation but eventually pull clear to safety. Forced to sack his former Ipswich Town colleague Mick Mills, he too lost his job when he refused to negotiate a new 'manager only' contract after the club chairman felt he should take a cut in salary as he was suffering from a long-term injury.

Butcher later became player/manager of Sunderland but was dismissed at the end of the 1992–93 season after the club had finished twenty first in the First Division.

He is now in charge of the Old Manor Hotel in Bridge of Allen near Stirling and still writes a weekly column in the *Scottish Daily Express* and gives regular commentaries on Sky Television.

C

CANTWELL, NOEL

Irish Schoolboy international Noel Cantwell joined West Ham United as a twenty-year-old in 1952. He made his Football League debut in April 1953 in a 3–2 win at Fulham. He was a major factor in the club's promotion-winning season of 1957–58 and was one of five ever-presents the following season – the club's first campaign back in the top flight. When he joined Manchester United for £29,500 in November 1960 it was a record fee for a full-back.. At Old Trafford he followed in a long line of captains and led the Reds to victory in the 1963 FA Cup Final. Towards the end of his career he concentrated on coaching but just when many people thought he would succeed Matt Busby, he replaced Jimmy Hill as manager of Coventry City.

Noel Cantwell.

Arriving at Highfield Road in October 1967 he saved the club from relegation although matters were not resolved until the final game of the season. The club struggled against relegation again in the following campaign but in 1969–70 Cantwell led it to a best finish of sixth in Division One and a place in Europe. Cantwell stayed with the Sky Blues until March 1972 when, following a 1–0 FA Cup defeat by Hull City, he was sacked.

Shortly afterwards he took over as manager of Peterborough United but in 1977 he left English soccer to manage the Boston Tea Men in the NASL. He returned to Peterborough in 1986, later becoming general manager, but parted comany with the club again in April 1989. A former PFA Chairman, the thirty six capped Republic of Ireland full-back also managed the national side for a while.

CAPACITY

The capacity of Highfield Road in 1999-2000 was 23,611.

CAPS

The most capped players in the club's history are Ronnie Rees of Wales and Dave Clements of Northern Ireland, both of whom had twenty one caps.

CAPS (ENGLAND)

The first Coventry City player to be capped by England was goalkeeper Reg Matthews when he played against Scotland in 1956. The City 'keeper, who later played for Chelsea and Derby County, is also the club's most capped player with five caps.

CAPS (NORTHERN IRELAND)

The first Coventry City player to be capped by Northern Ireland was Jackie Brown when he played against England in 1936. The most capped player is Dave Clements with twenty one caps.

CAPS (REPUBLIC OF IRELAND)

The first Coventry City player to be capped by the Republic of Ireland was Jackie Brown when he played against Switzerland in 1937. The most capped player is Jimmy Holmes with seventeen caps.

CAPS (SCOTLAND)

The first Coventry City player to be capped by Scotland was Willie Carr when he played against Northern Ireland in 1970. The most capped player is Tommy Hutchison with seventeen caps.

CAPS (WALES)

The first Coventry City player to be capped by Wales was Bob Evans when he played against Ireland in 1911. The most capped player is Ronnie Rees with twenty one caps.

CAPTAINS

During 1908–09, the club's first season in the Southern League, Charlie Tickle was not only appointed captain after a bad run of results but was even asked on one occasion to select the Coventry side for the next match at New Brompton. Coventry won 1–0 and Tickle scored the goal.

The club's first captain in the Football League was George Chaplin, a Scottish international who had joined the club from Bradford City in 1918. He was the key figure in the 'Bury Scandal' and in 1923 after appearing in 113 League and Cup games, was banned for life by the FA.

George Mason was Coventry's captain when they won their first major honour, the Third Division (South) Championship, in 1935–36. He later became the club's first England international, although his appearances were in two unofficial wartime matches. Mason appeared in 350 games before leaving the club in 1952 to play non-league football for Nuneaton Borough.

George Curtis skippered Coventry to their second Championship success in 1963–64 when the club won the Third Division title. Known as 'The Ironman', Curtis played in 538 games over fifteen seasons with the club that he later managed from April 1986 to May 1987.

The first Coventry City captain to lift the FA Cup was Brian Kilcline, who did so following the Sky Blues 3–2 win over Tottenham Hotspur in 1987. This England Under-21 international, one of the game's most inspirational captains, went on to score thirty five goals in 211 games before leaving Highfield Road to continue his career with Oldham Athletic.

CARR, WILLIE

Although born in Glasgow Willie Carr moved to Cambridge with his parents at the age of thirteen and was actually chosen for an England Schoolboys trial. After joining Coventry he graduated up through the ranks, first featuring in a star-studded Sky Blues youth side before eventually winning a first team place, coming on as a substitute for Brian Lewis in a 1–1 draw at Arsenal in September 1967.

The Coventry youngsters reached the FA Youth Cup Final in 1968 but Carr missed the final as he was in the first team at Southampton. By the start of the 1968–69 season he was an established member of the Coventry side and although not a prolific scorer he hit a hat-trick in a 3–0 home win over West Bromwich Albion in August 1969.

Although goals were not Willie Carr's forte he was famous for his part in the 'donkey-kick' free kick that was introduced to *Match of the Day* viewers in the autumn of 1970.

His performances in midfield led to him winning the first of six full caps for Scotland when he played against Northern Ireland in April 1970. He seemed certain to be chosen for Scotland's 1974 World Cup squad but badly injured his knee in a clash with Liverpool's Phil Boersma at Highfield Road. He returned to the Sky Blues side the following season but was obviously strug-

Willie Carr.

gling and after scoring thirty seven goals in 298 games he was allowed to join Wolves for the knockdown price of £80,000.

At the end of his first full season at Molineux Wolves were relegated, but after winning the Second Division Championship in 1976–77 they entered a 'purple period' in the club's history, reaching the FA Cup semi-final twice and winning the League Cup in the next three years.

After making more than 200 appearances for Wolves Carr left to join Millwall. However his stay at The Den was brief and he played non-league football for Worcester, Willenhall and Stourbridge before leaving the game.

CARVER, JESSE

Formerly a butcher's assistant, Carver made his name as a robust type of centre-half with Blackburn Rovers and Newcastle United. It was after the Second World War that he became more famous with his revolutionary ideas. He perfected his methods on the continent with the Dutch FA, Lazio and Juventus, whom he guided to the Serie 'A' Championship in 1950.

In May 1952 Carver returned to these shores as trainer/coach of West Bromwich Albion and although he returned to Italy and Lazio in February 1953, he had done a good job. The side he left behind finished fourth and in 1953–54, under Vic Buckingham, went close to lifting the double.

After managing Lazio, AS Roma, Genoa and Internazionale, Carver took over the reins of Coventry City in the summer of 1955. Sadly, his six months in charge at Highfield Road proved that continental-style football did not work in the Third Division. It was only after the team altered their style that results improved and in December the club won five successive matches.

He was released from his contract at the end of the year and returned to Italy to manage Lazio for a second time. He returned to England in 1958 as coach of Tottenham Hotspur but once again failed to settle and moved on to work in America and Portugal.

CATTLIN, CHRIS

Chris Cattlin arrived at Highfield Road from Huddersfield Town on the transfer deadline of 15 March 1968 for a fee of £70,000 – then a British record for a left-back. The following day he made his debut for the Sky Blues and was given the awesome task of marking George Best in the home match against Manchester United. The Irish international never got a look in as Coventry won 2–0. Early the following season he won the first of two caps at Under–23 level when he played for England against Wales.

Cattlin was a first team regular for the Sky Blues for eight seasons. appearing in 239 League and Cup games and though he did not score a goal, it was not for the want of trying. The tough-tackling defender was sent off twice in his Highfield Road career, although on the first occasion against Everton in 1971 he was mistaken for Jeff Blockley.

When he was given a free transfer at the end of the 1975–76 season City supporters collected a petition in the hope of making the club have a change of heart. It was all to no avail and Cattlin (pictured right) joined Brighton and Hove Albion. He helped the Seagulls rise from the Third to the First Division before retiring at the age of thirty two after a persistent Achilles tendon injury. He later managed the Sussex club before running a rock shop on the front at Brighton.

CENTURIES

Only two players have scored 100 or more league goals for Coventry Ciy. Clarrie Bourton is the greatest goalscorer with 171 strikes in his Highfield Road career. The other centurion is Billy Lake who netted 113 league goals.

Steve Ogrizovic and Alf Wood hold the club record for the most consecutive league appearances with 209. Other players to have made over 100 consecutive league appearances at any stage during their careers are Jerry Best (170), Bobby McDonald (160), George Curtis (153), Jack Astley (138), Roy Kirk (129), Jeff Blockley (108), George Curtis (107) and Tommy Hutchison (102).

CHAMPIONSHIPS

Coventry City have won a divisional championship on three occasions. In 1935–36 City won the Third Division (South) title, finishing one point ahead of runners-up Luton Town against whom they drew both games towards the end of the season. Coventry won nineteen and drew one of their twenty one home games, their only defeat being 2–0 at the hands of

Aldershot on Christmas Day. The club also had some big wins, beating Crystal Palace 8–1, Newport County 7–1 and Queen's Park Rangers 6–1.

Coventry's second Championship success came in 1963–64 when they won the Third Division title. They started the season with six wins and a draw in their opening seven fixtures. George Hudson was the club's top scorer with twenty four goals in thirty two matches, including a hat-trick in City's biggest win of the season, 6–3 at Queen's Park Rangers. He also scored the only goal of the game on the final day of the season against Colchester United which ensured Coventry won the Championship on goal average from Crystal Palace.

Coventry last won a divisional Championship in 1966–67 when they finished the campaign one point ahead of Wolverhampton Wanderers. Again the club only lost one home game, 2–1 to Crystal Palace; won fifteen; and drew ten of their last twenty five games. Bobby Gould was the leading scorer with twenty four goals in thirty nine games including a hat-trick in a 5–0 home win over Ipswich Town.

CHAPLIN, ALFRED

Alfred Chaplin played his early football for Foleshill Great Heath and, after impressing in a game in which he played at centre-half instead of his usual wing-half, he was selected for a trial by Birmingham Juniors. He joined Coventry during the 1902–03 season and made his debut in a 2–0 home win over Kidderminster Harriers. After just five appearances he left Highfield Road and joined Small Heath before signing for Woolwich Arsenal in 1905. However, after two years with the Gunners in which he failed to win a place in their first team, he rejoined Coventry. Over the next five seasons he was a virtual ever-present in the City side, going on to score eight goals in 193 games. In his last season with the club, 1911–12, he was granted a deserved testimonial against Chelsea in the South Eastern League.

CHARITY SHIELD

Coventry City's only appearance in the FA Charity Shield took place on 1 August 1987 when, following their FA Cup triumph, they played League Champions Everton in front of a Wembley crowd of 88,000. In a disappointing game Everton won 1–0 with Wayne Clarke scoring the Toffees' goal.

CHISHOLM, KEN

Ken Chisholm was a figher pilot during the Second World War. In 1945 he joined Queen's Park and the following year appeared for Scotland in a Victory international against Northern Ireland. On leaving Hampden Park he had a spell playing for Partick Thistle before, in January 1948, Major Frank Buckley signed him for Leeds United. His stay at Elland Road lasted less than a year as he moved to Leicester City. It was when he was with the Foxes that Chisholm won his only honour, an FA Cup runners-up medal in 1949.

In March 1950, Chisholm joined Coventry City and made his debut in a 1–1 draw at home to Blackburn Rovers. The following season of 1950–51 was his only complete season at Highfield Road. Chisholm was the club's top scorer with twenty four goals in thirty eight games with most of his strikes coming before the turn of the year. His total included his only hat-trick for the club in a 4–1 home defeat of Luton Town. He had taken his tally of goals to thirty five in seventy one games when, in March 1952, he was sold to Cardiff City. He scored eight goals in the last eleven games of the campaign to help the Bluebirds win promotion to the First Division. For the next two seasons he was the Ninian Park club's leading scorer, netting a hat-trick in October 1953 in a 5–0 home win over Charlton Athletic. He later played for Sunderland and Workington and in January 1958 became player/manager of Glentoran.

Chisholm was one of the players involved in the Sunderland illegal payments scandal of the 1950s. He was suspended *sine die* for refusing to answer the investigating committee's questions. Subsequently he admitted receiving illegal payments and forfeited his benefit qualification terms.

CLEAN SHEET

This is the colloquial expression used to describe a goalkeeper's performance when he does not concede a goal. Bill Morgan kept 17 clean sheets from 41 league appearances in 1938–39 when the club finished fourth in Division Two.

CLEMENTS, DAVE

The winner of forty eight Northern Ireland caps, Dave Clements began his career as a winger with Wolverhampton Wanderers. He failed to make the grade at Molineux and he joined Coventry City in the summer of 1964 for £1,000. After scoring on his debut in a 1–1 draw at Northampton in January 1965, Clements went on to score eight goals in his first ten games for the club. At Highfield Road Clements was converted into a half-back but after seven seasons with the club in which he scored thirty goals in 257 games, he left to join Sheffield Wednesday for a fee of £100,000.

At Hillsborough he played mainly at full-back. After appearing in seventy eight league games for the club he moved on to Everton for £60,000 in September 1973. He was one of the Goodison Park club's most intelligent players and he was playing for the Merseysiders against Middlesbrough in March 1975 when he learned he had been appointed manager of Northern Ireland. On leaving Everton he joined New York Cosmos. His decision to play in America cost him his job as his country's manager.

COLOURS

The club's present colours are Sky Blue and navy stripes with white side stripes, sky blue shorts and stockings. The club's change colours are purple and gold.

Between 1923 and 1925, Coventry played in red and green shirts, which were the town's civic colours. The shirt also sported an outsize coat of arms.

The Coventry City v Southend United match on 13 January 1962 had been in progress for three minutes before it was noticed that both teams were playing in blue and white. Referee Arthur Holland stopped play and Coventry changed into red shirts on the field.

CONSECUTIVE AWAY GAMES

Coventry City played seven consecutive away matches in Division One between home fixtures against Middlesbrough on 22 January 1977 and Tottenham Hotspur on 2 April 1977. They won the first of those matches,

2–1 at Leeds United but then drew one and lost five of the remaining fixtures. To make matters worse they drew both home matches played at either end of that sequence.

CONSECUTIVE HOME GAMES

Coventry City have played an extraordinary intense sequence of four home league games in succession on three occasions but in 1957–58 they played the four games in just fourteen days. They beat Aldershot 6–0 with both Jim Rogers and Peter Hill netting hat-tricks; Walsall 4–0 with Ray Straw scoring three goals; and drew the games against Queen's Park Rangers and Plymouth Argyle 1–1. For the record, the club were also unbeaten in both of the other sequences of four consecutive home league games.

CONSECUTIVE SCORING – LONGEST SEQUENCE

Clarrie Bourton holds the club record for consecutive scoring when he was on target in ten consecutive league games, scoring nineteen goals in the process. He scored his first two goals in a 4–0 home win over Exeter City on 19 September 1931 and the last in a 2–2 draw at Swindon Town on 21 November 1931.

COOP, MICK

Mick Coop joined Coventry City in 1963 and after a three–year apprentice ship turned professional in January 1966. After some impressive performances for the club's reserve side, he made his first team debut in a 3–1 League Cup defeat at the hands of Brighton and Hove Albion in October 1966. However, it was 1968–69 before he established himself as a regular member of the City side.

He was appointed the club's penalty–taker and in February 1973 scored his first goal for the club from the penalty–spot in a 1–0 FA Cup win over Grimsby Town. That season Coop was ever-present whilst in 1973–74 he had his best season in terms of goals scored, netting seven in 41 appearances including two penalties in a 2–2 home draw against Chelsea.

When Graham Oakey replaced Coop in the Sky Blues' side in 1974–75

Coop spent six months on loan at York City, but played in just four league games for the Bootham Crescent club. On his return to Highfield Road he switched from full-back to central defender.

Mick Coop.

He went on to score twenty two goals from 499 League and Cup games before leaving to play for Derby County.

Unable to settle at the Baseball Ground, his contract was cancelled and early in 1982 he left to play non-league football for AP Leamington.

Coop later returned to Highfield Road as City's youth team coach and in 1987 led the Sky Blues to success in the FA Youth Cup. Two years later following a row with manager John Sillett, Coop left the club.

CRICKETERS

Coventry City have had six players or managers who were also cricketers of distinction.

Patsy Hendren, small, stocky with a ready London wit, was loved by crowds and deeply respected by opposing bowlers as a master craftsman. Once at a cricket dinner he accidentally knocked over his chair as he rose to speak and immediately quipped: 'That's by no means the first time I've heard the sound of falling timber behind me.' Hendren's career had begun as early as 1907 and he did not completely retire until 1938. He played for England in fifty one Tests and he scored 40,302 runs for his county, Middlesex, at a batting average of 48.82. On his debut for Coventry on 30 October 1909, he scored twice in a 3–0 win at Watford and kept his place for the rest of the season scoring thirteen goals in twenty nine games. He damaged his knee at the start of the 1910–11 season and after appearing in a handful of games, left to join Brentford.

Harry Storer, who had two spells managing Coventry leading them to the Third Division Championship in 1935–36, played county cricket for

Derbyshire. A hard-hitting batsman, he scored 13,513 runs at 27.63 and captured 232 wickets. Another Derbyshire player was Charlie Elliott who joined Coventry from Chesterfield in 1931. Although he remained at Highfield Road until 1948, he only made 101 League and Cup appearances due to the consistency of the other players in his position. For Derbyshire he scored 11,965 runs at 27.25 and after becoming a first class umpire, stood in forty six Tests.

Warwickshire's Freddie Gardner played in 338 matches for the county, scoring 17,826 runs at an average of 33.83. His highest score was 215 not out against Somerset at Taunton in 1950. He was the scorer of twenty nine centuries and he also hit 1,000 runs in a season on ten occasions. For Coventry he only made eighteen appearances, following his transfer from Birmingham City, before leaving to continue his career with Newport County.

Don Bennett of Middlesex was a player of great ability. He scored 10,274 runs and took 748 wickets with his fast/medium deliveries and was a valuable member of the county side. He joined Coventry from Arsenal in September 1959 and served the club well for three seasons, appearing in seventy seven games.

Another Coventry player to turn out at county level was Jack Lee of Leicestershire. He joined City from Derby County and in eighteen games in 1954–55 scored ten goals.

CURTIS, GEORGE

A tough uncompromising defender, George Curtis joined Coventry City from Snowdown Colliery in October 1955 and made his debut at the end of that season in a 4–3 defeat at Newport County. By the start of the 1958–59 season Curtis, who was known as 'The Ironman', had established himself at the heart of the Coventry defence. Over the next nine seasons he missed very few games and was ever-present in 1960–61, 1961–62, 1963–64, 1965–66 and 1966–67.

He was the foundation stone to the club's success and after helping it win promotion from the Fourth Division in 1958–59, captained the Sky Blues to the Third Division Championship in 1963–64 and the Second Division title in 1966–67. In only his second match in the top flight, a

3–3 draw at Nottingham Forest, Curtis broke his leg. He tried to make a number of comebacks but was now behind Roy Barry and Jeff Blockley in the pecking order.

Curtis, who had scored thirteen goals in 538 games, joined Aston Villa for £25,000 but after a short stay at Villa Park returned to Highfield Road to work in the club's commercial department. He later became the club's managing director and also its team manager and, after helping the Sky Blues avoid relegation in 1985–86, teamed up with John Sillett to take the club to its first FA Cup Final.

D

DEBUTS

George Hudson scored a hat-trick on his Coventry debut on 6 April 1963 as the Sky Blues beat Halifax Town 5–4. He went on to score seventy five goals in 129 games before leaving to join Northampton Town.

There was nothing eventful about Ernie Boston's debut in a 5–2 home defeat by Southend United on 26 September 1908, except that he should have played his first game for the club at Millwall a week earlier. The reason young Boston did not play in that game was that he forgot to bring his boots.

DEFEATS – FEWEST

During the 1966–67 season Coventry City went through the forty two match programme and suffered only six defeats on their way to winning the Second Division Championship.

DEFEATS – MOST

A total of twenty two defeats in the seasons of 1919–20, 1924–25, 1927–28, 1951–52 and 1984–85 is the worst in the club's history. Surprisingly, Coventry City were only relegated in two of those campaigns, 1924–25 and 1951–52.

DEFEATS – WORST

Coventry City' record defeat in the Football League was when Norwich City beat them 10–2 in a Third Division (South) game on 15 March 1930. The club had earlier been beaten 9–1 by Millwall on 19 November 1927. The Sky Blues worst defeat in the FA Cup was when Berwick Rangers beat them 11–2 in a qualifying round of the competition.

DEFENSIVE RECORDS

Coventry City's best defensive record was established in 1970–71 when the club finished tenth in the First Division. The side conceded thirty eight goals in that campaign of forty two matches.

The Sky Blues' worst defensive record was in 1931–32 when they let in nine goals. This happened in the same season in which they scored their highest number of league goals – a total of 108.

DENNISON, BOB

After playing at inside-left for both Newcastle United and Nottingham Forest, Bob Dennison joined Fulham where he was converted to centre-half. During the Second World War he guested for Northampton Town and after signing for them on a permanent basis became their manager in 1948. He left the County Ground in 1954 to take charge of Middlesbrough. It was Dennison who 'discovered' Brian Clough but in nine years at Ayresome Park he failed to win promotion for the Teeside club. In December 1963, with nineteen months of his contract still to run, he was asked to leave. He took the club to the High Court where he won damages of £3,200 for 'unfair dismissal'.

After going into non-league management with Hereford United he joined Coventry City as chief scout in December 1967. Following Noel Cantwell's dismissal, Dennison was made caretaker-maanger for the last twelve games of the 1971–72 season. When Joe Mercer and Gordon Milne arrived on the scene he was appointed assistant-manager and he retained his involvement with the club's scouting system.

DISMISSALS

One of the first Coventry players to be sent off was 'gentleman' goalkeeper Teddy Kirk. In a game against Small Heath just before the turn of the century he was sent off for knocking a Birmingham forward unconcious with a powerful uppercut.

Chris Cattlin was sent off twice during his Highfield Road career. The first occasion was a mistake. When the Sky Blues played Everton at Goodison Park on 2 October 1971 he was mistaken for Jeff Blockley.

Mick Quinn holds the unenviable record of being the first Coventry player to be dismissed in a Premier League match. He was sent off when the Sky Blues played Blackburn Rovers at Ewood Park on 27 August 1994. He had also been sent off in the match against Manchester United on 12 April 1993 but following video evidence his dismissal was removed from the record books.

DIVISION THREE (SOUTH) CUP

The Division Three North and South Cups were started in 1933–34. The club's first opponents that season were Bristol Rovers who were beaten 2–1 after the first meeting had ended all square at 2–2. Following a 3–1 win over Southend United, City met Exeter in the semi-final. A Clarrie Bourton goal helped Coventry draw 1–1 at St James Park but despite having most of the game in the replay at Highfield Road, the Grecians won 1–0.

In 1934–35 Coventry beat Bournemouth 5–2 at Dean Court and then defeated Crystal Palace 5–1 with Clarrie Bourton scoring a hat-trick. The club's opponents in the semi-final were Watford but after City were held to a 1–1 draw at home, the Hornets won the replay at Vicarage Road 2–1.

The club last participated in the competition in 1935–36 when it won the trophy. After beating Millwall (Away 1–0) and Bournemouth (Home 3–2), City beat Crystal Palace 2–1 at Selhurst Park in the semi-final to win a place in that season's final against Swindon Town. Goals from Frith and Lauderdale gave City a 2–0 win at the County Ground and a 3–2 victory in the second leg at Highfield Road ensured that Coventry won the trophy 5–2 on aggregate.

DOUGALL, JIMMY

A Scottish junior international, winger Jimmy Dougall was signed for Coventry by manager Harry Pollitt midway through the 1919–20 season and made his debut in a 4–3 defeat at Rotherham County on 17 January 1920. He missed very few games over the next six seasons during which time his accurate crosses provided a number of goal scoring opportunities for, among others, Sam Stevens and Albert Pynegar. His performances for City led to a number of top clubs showing an interest and on one occasion the club rejected a bid of £2,000 from Manchester United.

Dougall went on to score fourteen goals in 237 League and Cup games before leaving Highfield Road to join Reading. Sadly he had only appeared in twelve games for the then Elm Park club before he broke his leg – an injury which effectively ended his career in first class football..

DOWNS, GREG

A natural left-footer with the ability to overlap, Greg Downs began his career with Norwich City but made his league debut when on loan to

Torquay United. On his return to Carrow Road he was converted into a fine left-back and made his first team debut for the Canaries in a League Cup tie at Burnley in August 1979. However, it was another two seasons before he won a regular place in the Norwich side. In 1981–82, when the Canaries won promotion to the First Division, Downs won all the Player of the Year awards and in 1982–83 was one of two ever-presents as the Norwich strove to consolidate themselves in the top flight. Downs appeared in all fifty three of the club's matches in 1983–84 but in the summer of 1985, after being left out of the Norwich League Cup Final side, he joined Coventry City for £40,000.

Greg Downs.

Downs was bought to replace Stuart Pearce, who had left to join Nottingham Forest, and made his debut in a 1–1 home draw against Manchester City on the opening day of the 1985–86 season. He came in for a lot of criticism in his first season at Highfield Road but he won the fans over and became one of the club's most popular players. When City won the FA Cup in 1987 Downs contributions in the five matches to the final were outstanding and in the final itself he kept dangerman, Chris Waddle, quiet. there were a number of occasions. During his five seasons with the Sky Blues there were a number of occasions when he was on the verge of leaving the club but stayed to score seven goals in 181 League and Cup games.

In the summer of 1990 he joined Birmingham City on a free transfer and was made captain under Dave Mackay's managership. At the end of the 1990–91 season he left St Andrew's to become player/coach at Hereford United.

DRAWS

Coventry City played their greatest number of drawn league matches in a single season in 1962–63 when seventeen of their matches ended all square. The club's highest scoring draw is 5–5, notched up against Fulham (Home 2 January 1932) and Southampton (Away 4 May 1982).

DUBLIN, DION

Dion Dublin was playing for non-league Oakham Town, a works team based in Sutton-in-Ashfield, when he was spotted by Norwich City in March 1988. However, despite signing professional forms for the Canaries, he was released during the summer and joined Fourth Division Cambridge United on a non-contract basis. Following a trial period, he made his Football League debut as a substitute in a 3–1 defeat at Wrexham on 16 December 1988. In only his second full appearance for the club, he scored a hat-trick in a 5–1 victory at Peterborough. In 1989–90 he topped the club's scoring charts and helped it reach the sixth round of the FA Cup as well as qualifying for the play-offs. It eventually won promotion after beating Chesterfield 1–0 at Wembley with Dublin scoring the only goal. In 1990–91 Cambridge won the Third Division Championship and again reached the sixth round of the FA Cup. Dublin was once again the club's top scorer with twenty one goals. In 1991–92 Cambridge looked to be going all the way to the top flight but were beaten by Leicester City in the play-offs.

Downs had scored seventy four goals in 202 games for Cambridge when Manchester United manager, Alex Ferguson, paid £1 million to take him to Old Trafford. He scored the winning goal in the last minute of his full debut at Southampton and then broke his leg in only his sixth game at home to Crystal Palace. Following the arrival of Eric Cantona, he found it difficult to win a regular place and in September 1994 he joined Coventry City for £2 million.

He scored on his debut in a 2–2 draw at Queen's Park Rangers and ended the season as the club's top scorer with sixteen goals. Appointed club captain, he had another good goal scoring season in 1995–96, netting a hat-trick in a 4–3 defeat by Sheffield Wednesday at Hillsborough in his total of sixteen goals. The following season he lost the captaincy and, after beings sent off in successive games, suffered a seven-match ban. In 1997–98 Dublin had an outstanding season, winning his first England cap against Chile at Wembley. He was the club's leading scorer for the fourth year running, his total of twenty three goals including a first day hat-trick in a 3–2 win over Chelsea.

Dublin had scored sixty eight goals in 159 games for Coventry when Aston Villa paid £5.75 million for his services in the summer of 1998. After a sensational start to his Villa career, injury brought his first season at Villa Park to a premature end, though he returned to help Villa reach the FA Cup Final in 2000.

E

EARLY GROUNDS

After beginning life in 1883 as Singer's FC the team first played on Dowells Field, between St George's Road and the railway line, before moving to their first enclosed ground on Stoke Road in 1887. It was another nine years before any ground improvements were made and these amounted to the provision of what was described as 'stout fences' around the pitch.

A year later in 1897, the club had to move the pitch some 50 yards to the east to allow for the extension of King Richard Street. This proved to be a temporary measure and in 1899, when the ground was acquired for building, Singers FC – which by now had become Coventry City – began making preparations for a new ground on a field just 100 yards away then being used by the Craven Cricket Club.

ELLIOTT, CHARLIE

After failing to make the grade with Sheffield Wednesday, the versatile Elliott joined Coventry City but over the next sixteen seasons he only appeared in 101 games.

After a a spell out of the game he returned to Highfield Road as the club's chief scout discovering, among others, Ray Sambrook who was later sold to Manchester City for £15,000. When Jack Fairbrother resigned in October 1954 the Coventry board appointed Elliott as the club's caretaker/manager until the arrival of Jesse Carver the following summer. Elliott then reverted to the role of chief scout, but lost his post six months later.

Charlie Elliott was also a fine opening batsman for Derbyshire, scoring 11,965 runs in seven seasons. He was later a Test umpire and chairman of Derbyshire's cricket committee.

EVANS, ALBERT

Albert Evans spent ten years with Aston Villa, winning three League Championships and an FA Cup winners' medal. He had the misfortune to break his leg five times – three times with Villa; once with West Bromwich Albion which he joined in 1906; and once in a charity game in 1915. Forming one of Villa's youngest full-back pairings with Howard Spencer, Evans went on to play in 203 League and Cup games before joining the Baggies.

Although he never gained international recognition he represented the Football League against the Irish League in 1900. After three years playing for West Bromwich Albion, he became their trainer, taking over as manager of Coventry City in 1920.

During his four years at Highfield Road, it was a constant struggle and the club were lucky to survive relegation with Evans at the helm. It was struggling under a mountain of debt and Evans inherited only a moderate team. Despite strengthening the side, Coventry's highest position was eighteenth in the Second Division, yet both the players and the supporters were loyal to him.

Evans 'resigned' in 1924 and travelled the world, trying a variety of jobs including prospecting for gold in the Yukon.

EVER-PRESENTS

There have been thirty eight Coventry City players who have been ever-present throughout a league season. The greatest number of ever-present seasons by a Sky Blues player is six by Steve Ogrizovic. Next in line comes George Curtis with five and Alf Wood with four.

F

FA CUP

Coventry City's early association with the FA Cup was very much hit or miss. In 1900–01 they withdrew against Oswestry Town to fulfil a league fixture and might have been better advised to find a similar excuse the following season. They lost 11–2 to Berwick Rangers and even one of their two goals was scored by an opponent.

The club's first made an impact on the FA Cup competition in 1909–10 when they were still members of the Southern League. They reached the fourth round, beating First Division Preston North End (Away 2–1) and Nottingham Forest (Home 3–1) before losing 2–0 at home to another top flight club in Everton.

It was 1962–63 before City, then a Third Division club, had another good FA Cup run. After beating Bournemouth (Home 1–0), Millwall (Home 2–1 after a goal-less draw) and Lincoln City (Away 5–1) they met Portsmouth in round four. After two draws City won the third meeting at White Hart Lane to set up a fifth round tie at home to Sunderland. A crowd of 40,487 saw Coventry come back from 1–0 down to win 2–1 with goals from Bruck and Curtis in a frantic final eight minutes. In the quarter-final, Coventry lost 3–1 to eventual FA Cup winners, Manchester United.

In 1986–87 the Sky Blues reached their first FA Cup Final, beating Bolton Wanderers (Home 3–0), Manchester United (Away 1–0), Stoke City (Away 1–0) and Sheffield Wednesday (Away 3–1) to set up a semi-final meeting against Leeds United at Hillsborough. The Yorkshire side took the lead but Cyrille Regis wasted three good chances to level the scores before half-time. Gynn equalised after coming on as a substitute before Houchen shot the Sky Blues ahead. Leeds equalised in the 83rd minute to send the game into extra time. City won the game after eight minutes of extra time when Dave Bennett followed up Houchen's shot that Mervyn Day had been unable to hold. In the final, the Sky Blues twice came from behind to beat Tottenham Hotspur 3–2 and win the FA Cup for the first time in their history.

Two years later eight of the club's winning squad were on duty at Sutton United's Gander Green Lane when the mid-table Vauxhall Conference side beat them 2–1. Since then Coventry's best performance in the FA Cup has been to reach the sixth round in 1998–99 where they lost 3–1 on penalties to Sheffield United after both games had ended 1–1.

FA CUP FINAL

On 16 May 1987 Coventry City appeared in their first FA Cup Final against Tottenham Hotspur. The game was only two minutes old when Chris Waddle picked up a woefully weak clearance, beat Greg Downs, and crossed to the far post where Clive Allen put Spurs 1–0 up. But within seven minutes Coventry were level. A cross from Greg Downs was not cleared and Dave Bennett whipped the ball from the hesitant Steve Hodge to steer it past Ray Clemence. Four minutes from half-time Glenn Hoddle's free kick sailed over the stranded Steve Ogrizovic for the hapless Brian Kilcline to get the final touch as Gary Mabbutt thundered in. Bennett's cross in the 63rd minute eluded the Spurs defence and Keith Houchen scored with a superb diving header. There was no further scoring in the 90 minutes and so the game went into extra time. In the 96th minute, Gary Mabbutt in his attempt to clear Lloyd McGrath's cross, merely deflected the ball into his own net. It was a remarkable triumph for the Sky Blues and just reward for the management duo of George Curtis and John Sillett.

The Coventry team was: S Ogrizovic, D Phillips, G Downs, L McGrath, B Kilcline (G Rodger), T Peake, D Bennett, M Gynn, C Regis, K Houchen and N Pickering.

FA INQUIRY

After ten years of successful Southern League membership, Coventry were voted into the Second Division of the Football League for the 1919–20 season.

However, after forty matches the club had won only eight, and with two games left – Bury home and awa – at least three points were needed if City were to avoid finishing in the bottom two. One of the re-election places was already occupied by Grimsby Town, the other was to be contested by Coventry and Lincoln.

Bury were in fifth position and so Coventry supporters hoped that the Gigg Lane club would have little to play for, especially as Tottenham Hotspur were already assured of First Division football the following season.

The trip to Lancashire on the penultimate Saturday saw City draw 2–2, courtesy of goals from Wynn and Lowes. Seven days later, a crowd of 23,506 flocked to Highfield Road to see if City could complete the job. By half–time, the Shakers led 1–0 as Coventry produced easily their worst performance of the season. It could so easily have been four or five but the Lancashire club let City off the hook time and time again. There was a marked improvement in Coventry's form in the second half and although the visitors should have extended their lead, two goals from Mercer who had joined the club from Bury at the start of the season, brough City a 2–1 victory.

Bury's excuse for their poor form was that they had lost their kit on the way to the game and although City lent them another, the boots had proved to be a poor fit.

Lincoln lost their league status, having failed to secure the necessary votes for re–election. Rumours abounded for a number of months and eventually the FA started an inquiry.

George Chaplin, captain of the Coventry side, had travelled to Bury a few days prior to the start of the first game between the clubs. With £200 he managed to 'buy off' a number of Bury players. It was their performances that led to Coventry eventually avoiding the drop. However, at a later interview Chaplin recalled that a Bury player had said that the Coventry players were so bad in the second game they he and his team mates had trouble playing badly enough to allow the Coventry side a victory.

At the end of the FA inquiry five Bury players, two directors and an official, plus the Coventry chairman, director Jack Marshall and captain George Chaplin were all banned. Two years later, Coventry manager Harry Pollitt was suspended *sine die*. There were calls for the Midlands side to be thrown out of the League and rumours persisted for a good number of seasons after if ever a game looked suspect.

FAIRBROTHER, JACK

Jack Fairbrother played his early football for Burton Town before joining Preston North End as a youthful but promising stand-in for the dependable Harry Holdcroft. After having had to be content with Central League football until the outbreak of war he eventually made his league debut for the Deepdale club in August 1946 in a 3–2 win over Leeds United. He played in forty one games in 1946–47 but at the end of the season he was sold to Newcastle United for £7,000. He played in 145 games for the Magpies and appeared in their 1951 FA Cup Final victory over Blackpool. After breaking his collar bone the popular goalkeeper went into management with non-league Peterborough United. His success at London Road led to him being appointed Coventry City manager in December 1953.

In 1953–54 the club finished fourteenth. A number of experienced players joined City in the close season nd they went to the top of the Third Division early in the 1954–55 campaign. Sadly injuries led to a poor run of results and, after only ten months in charge, Jack Fairbrother resigned. After managing Consett and Gateshead, he returned to Peterborough for a second spell and in 1962–63 led them to sixth place in Division Three.

FARMER, RON

Guernsey-born half-back Ron Farmer joined the Sky Blues as part of the double signing with goalkeeper Arthur Lightening from Nottingham Forest. He made his debut in a 5–1 home win over Chester in November 1958 and soon settled into the side. At the end of the season in which he had played twenty six games and scored his first goal for the club in a 3–2 win over Crewe, the Sky Blues were promoted to the Third Division.

In 1963–64, his best season for the club in terms of goals scored – eleven in forty four games including a hat-trick in a 5–1 win over Crystal Palace on the opening day of the season – he won a Third Division Championship medal. Farmer was still a regular member of the Coventry side in 1966–67 when they won the Second Division Championship but after just four appearances in the top flight, he was allowed to leave Highfield Road.

Farmer, who had scored fifty three goals in 315 League and Cup games, joined Notts County but after two seasons at Meadow Lane he left to play non-league football for Grantham Town. He later returned to Highfield Road as the club's youth team coach.

FATHER AND SON

Tony Hateley and his son Mark both played for Coventry City. Both players were much-travelled centre-forwards. Tony started his career with Notts County and later played for Aston Villa, Chelsea and Liverpool before arriving at Highfield Road. He scored five goals in twenty League and Cup games before joining Birmingham City and then moving on to play for Notts County again and Oldham Athletic. Tony Hateley scored 201 goals in 444 league games for his seven clubs. Mark Hateley joined the club as an apprentice and in five seasons in City's first team, scored thrity goals in 111 games including a hat-trick in a 5–5 draw at Southampton. He went on to win thirty two caps for England in a career in which he played for Portsmouth, Glasgow Rangers, AC Milan, AS Monaco, Queen's Park Rangers, Leeds United and Hull City.

Bobby Gould, who both played and managed the Sky Blues, was followed into the Coventry team by his goalkeeping son Jonathan who went on to make twenty seven first team appearances before leaving to play for Bradford City. Coventry City manager Gordon Strachan who played in fifty internationals for Scotland and has won domestic honours with Aberdeen, Manchester United and Leeds United, introduced his son Gavin into the Sky Blues' side in December 1997. Since then the Scotland Under-21 international has appeared in twelve Premier League games.

FERGUSON, MICK

A powerfully-built striker, Mick Ferguson played his first game for the Sky Blues in a goal-less draw at Leeds United in February 1975. In the next two seasons Ferguson appeared in just twenty nine games, scoring six goals, but at the start of the 1976–77 season his six goals in the first nine games led to him winning a regular place in the side. In 1977–78, when City finished seventh in Division One, Ferguson was the club's leading scorer with seventeen goals in thirty league games. His total included three hat-tricks against Manchester City (Home 4–2), Wolves (Away 3–1) and Birmingham City (Home 4–0). It was a remarkable performance because the Newcastle-born striker had two spells out through injury. Sadly, further injuries and a loss of form restricted his appearances over the next three seasons, although he did score four goals in a 4–1 win over Ipswich Town in December 1978 and in the summer of 1981 he joined Everton for £280,000.

Unable to settle at Goodison Park, he joined Birmingham City. He was top scorer in his first season at St Andrew's but further injuries kept him out of the side for long periods the following year. Towards the end of the 1983–84 season he returned to Highfield Road on loan and scored some vital goals to help keep Coventry in the First Division. Ferguson, who scored fifty sevengoals in 149 games in his two spells, later played for Brighton and Colchester United before playing non-league football for Wealdstone.

FIRST DIVISION

The club's only spell in the First Division began in 1967–68 and lasted for twenty five seasons until reorganisation in 1992–93 when City became members of the Premier League. During that time, the club's best position in the First Diviison was sixth in 1969–70 although it did finish seventh in seasons 1977–78 and 1988–89. In 1969–70, City won ten of their twenty one away games, a club record.

FIRST LEAGUE MATCH

Coventry City's first Football League match took place on 30 August 1919 when they entertained Tottenham Hotspur at Highfield Road. A crowd of 16,500 saw the visitors take the lead through Bert Bliss. Spurs went on to win 5–0 with Chipperfield (2) Grimsdell and Bliss again, the scorers. It took Coventry ten games before they secured their first point and twenty games before they won a League game, beating Stoke 3–2 on Christmas Day, having scored just four goals in nineteen games.

The Coventry team that day was: A E Lindon, R E Roberts, G D Chaplin, J Allan, F Hawley, H Clarke, L Sheldon, A Mercer, C L Sambrooke, T Lowes and F T B Gibson.

FLOODLIGHTS

The Highfield Road floodlights were first switched on for a friendly against Queen of the South on 21 October 1953, a match watched by a crowd of 16,923. The floodlights had been installed on poles but four years later the club sold them to Crewe Alexandra and replaced them with lights mounted on pylons. Third Lanark, another Scottish side, were City's opponents when the new lights, which had cost £15,000 and been paid for by the Supporters' Club, were first used.

During the 1993–94 season the corner floodlight pylons were replaced by lights mounted along both side stand roofs.

FOOTBALL LEAGUE CUP

Sad to relate, with the exception of 1980–81 and 1989–90 when the club reached the semi-final stage of the competition, Coventry City have had little luck in the League Cup.

The club's first match in the competition was on 10 October 1960 when a crowd of 6,643 saw them beat Barrow 4–2 at Highfield Road. It suffered its heaviest defeat in the competition when Leicester City won 8–1 at Highfield Road in December 1964. That match was a fifth round tie, a stage of the competition City also reached in 1970–71, 1973–74 and 1990–91. Coventry first reached the semi-final in 1980–81. After beating Manchester United 2–0 on aggregate, the Sky Blues beat Brighton (Away 2–1) Cambridge United (Away 1–0 after a 1–1 draw) Watford (Home 5–0 after a 2–2 draw) but then lost 4–3 on aggregate to West Ham United after winning the Highfield Road leg of the competition 3–2. Coventry reached the semi-final again in 1989–90. Following a 4–3 aggregate win over Grimsby Town they beat Queen's Park Rangers (Away 2–1), Manchester City (Away 1–0) and Sunderland (Home 5–0 after a goal-less draw) before meeting Nottingham Forest. After losing the first leg at the City Ground 2–1, the Sky Blues were held to a goal-less draw at Highfield Road.

FORMATION

The club were formed in 1883 by workers at Singer's bicycle factory and first played under the title Singer's FC. Its first success was to win the

Birmingham Junior Cup in 1891 and this led to it winning election to the Birmingham and District League in 1894. Four years later it acquired its current name and in 1908 joined the Southern League.

FOURTH DIVISION

Coventry City have spent just one season in the Fourth Division and that was 1958–59 when they finished runners-up to Port Vale and won promotion at the first attempt. City lost just one of their twenty three home games, 2–1 to Carlisle United, and Straw and Rogers netted forty goals. Rogers scored four goals in a 7–1 win over Aldershot, a match in which Straw scored the other three and a hat-trick in the return fixture which Coventry won 4–1. Not to be outdone, George Stewart netted four goals in a 6–1 win at Carlisle United – a perfect revenge for the club's only home defeat.

FRITH, BILLY

At the start of his career Sheffield-born wing-half Billy Frith was a part-time professional with Mansfield Town before moving to Chesterfield in 1930. After only a few appearances for the Spireites, Frith was badly injured and when he failed to regain full fitness was given a free transfer. Coventry manager Harry Storer took a chance on him and he made his debut against Newport County in September 1932, scoring one of the goals in a 3–1 win. However, it was 1934–35 before he established himself as a first team regular and he held his place up until the outbreak of the Second World War.

During the hostilities he continued to play for the Highfield Road club and guested for Leicester City.

In 1945 he was appointed player/manager of Port Vale but his stay with the Valiants was short-lived and he returned to Coventry to take his tally of first team appearances to 177 in which he scored four goals. Frith, who was Dick Bayliss' assistant, became City's manager when Bayliss died but when things began to go wrong for the club he was replaced by Harry Storer. Frith was very bitter at the way he had been treated and entered the teaching profession while also working as part-time manager of Rugby Town and later Stafford Rangers.

In 1955 he returned to Highfield Road to coach the juniors before two years later being appointed manager for a second time. In 1958–59 he took the club out of the Fourth Division but then things again went wrong and after City were beaten 2–1 by non-league King's Lynn in the 1961–62 FA Cup competition he was sacked along with his entire management team.

FULL MEMBERS' CUP

In 1985–86 the competition was run on a group basis with the winners of the eight groups qualifying for regional semi-finals. City faced Second Division opposition in Stoke City and Millwall but failed to beat either team, losing 3–0 at the Victoria Ground against Stoke and drawing 1–1 at home to Millwall.

In 1986–87 the competition was run on a knockout basis. After receiving a bye in the first round, Coventry lost 2–1 at Norwich City with David Phillips scoring their goal from the penalty spot.

G

GIBSON, IAN

Ian Gibson was just fifteen when he made his league debut for Accrington Stanley but after scoring three goals in nine games for the Peel Park club he was transferred to Bradford Park Avenue, another club that was to lose its league status. Gibson spent two years with the Yorkshire club, scoring eighteen goals in eighty eight league games before Middlesbrough paid £30,000 for his services in March 1962.

A former Scottish schoolboy international, he was capped at Under-23 level when at Ayresome Park but could do nothing to halt Boro's slide into the Third Division. Gibson had scored forty four goals in 168 games for the north-east club when Coventry City paid a record £57,500 to take him to Highfield Road. He made his debut in a 1–0 home win over Hull City on the opening day of the 1966–67 season and went on to score eight goals in thirty one games as the Sky Blues won the Second Division Championship. In the next two seasons his number of first team appearances were restricted due to a bad knee injury. He returned to the side on a regular basis in 1969–70 but in the summer of 1970, after scoring fourteen goals in 104 games, he was surprisingly sold to Cardiff City for £35,000.

Gibson, who helped the Bluebirds win the Welsh Cup in his first season at Ninian Park, scoring one of the goals in a 3–1 win over Wrexham, netted eighteen goals in 118 games before leaving to join Bournemouth in a £100,000 deal. Within twelve months of his arrival at Dean Court, he was forced to quit the game through injury.

GIBSON, TERRY

Terry Gibson won England youth honours while with Spurs where he developed through the ranks to make his league debut against Stoke City in December 1979 when still an apprentice. Despite proving a handful to the majority of opposing defenders he was unable to maintain a regular place in the Spurs side and in August 1983 he joined Coventry City for £100,000.

He made his Sky Blues debut at Watford on the opening day of the 1983–84 season, scoring one of the goals in a 3–2 win. He ended the season as the club's top scorer with nineteen goals, including a hat-trick in a 4–0 home win over Liverpool. He headed the club's scoring charts again the following season and in 1985–86, but after scoring fifty two goals in 113 games he was transferred to Manchester United. Sadly he never had an opportunity to prove himself at Old Trafford and after a miserable eighteen months he returned south to sign for Wimbledon for £200,000.

At the end of his first season with the Dons he had won an FA Cup winners' medal following Wimbledon's surprise 1–0 win over Liverpool in the Wembley final.

Terry Gibson.

Over the next four seasons Gibson helped the Dons establish themselves in the top flight but after being hampered by injuries left to play for Swindon Town. He later became player/coach at Barnet before severing his connections with the game.

GILLESPIE, GARY

Stirling-born defender Gary Gillespie was captain of Falkirk when Coventry manager, Gordon Milne, paid £75,000 to bring him to Highfield Road. Gillespie made his debut for the Sky Blues in a 2–1 win at Middlesbrough on the opening day of the 1978–79 season. He missed very few games over the next five seasons, being ever-present in 1982–83, his last season with the club. When with Coventry Gillespie, who appeared in 201 games, made eight appearances for Scotland at Under-21 level.

Gary Gillespie

He left Coventry for Liverpool in July 1983, after the Merseysiders had paid £325,000 for his services. During his years at Anfield, Gillespie won two League Championship medals and a number of runners-up medals. He formed a formidable defensive partnership with Alan Hansen but sadly he was susceptible to injury and this restricted the number of his appearances for the Anfield club.

Gillespie, who won thirteen caps for Scotland, left Liverpool in the summer of 1991 to join Glasgow Celtic for £1 million.

GLAZIER, BILL

Goalkeeper Bill Glazier began his Football League career with Crystal Palace and in three seasons with the Selhurst Park club made 106 league appearances.

In October 1964 City manager Jimmy Hill paid a world record fee of £35,000 for a goalkeeper to bring the Nottingham-born Glazier to Highfield Road. He kept a clean sheet on his debut as the Sky Blues beat Portsmouth 2–0 at Fratton Park and went on to be the club's first-choice 'keeper for the next ten seasons. He seemed to have a good chance of being selected for England's World Cup squad in 1966 but in April 1965 he broke his leg in a 1–1 draw at Manchester City and was out of the game for twelve months.

In 1966–67 Glazier missed just one game as the Sky Blues won the Second Division Championship, keeping thirteen clean sheets. There is no doubt that his performances during the club's first season in the top flight saved them from an immediate return to Second Division football.

He was one of the most popular 'keepers ever to play for City and he had made 402 first team appearances for the club when he lost his place to his understudy, Neil Ramsbottom, in the 1974–75 season. He left Highfield Road to play for Brentford but after just nine league games for the Bees he was forced to retire from the game due to another injury.

GOALKEEPERS

Coventry City used three different goalkeepers in three successive matches in 1979 and not one of them conceded a goal. On 28 August Jim Blyth kept goal in the League Cup second round first leg match at Portman Road against Ipswich Town which Coventry won 1–0. On 1 September, during the warm up before the start of the Division One game with Norwich City at Highfield Road, Blyth injured his back during the kickabout and was unable to take any part in the match. He was replaced just before the kick-off by Steve Murcott who on the same morning had played in goal for the club's youth team. It was Murcott's debut and he was able to keep a clean sheet in a 2–0 win. For the return League Cup game with Ipswich at Highfield Road on 4 September, Coventry had Les Sealey on duty between the posts in a goal-less draw.

GOALS

The most goals Coventry City have scored in one game was their 11–2 victory over West Bromwich Albion Reserves on the final day of the 1907–08 Birmingham and District League campaign. The club twice scored ten goals, beating Newport County 10–1 in the Southern League campaign of 1914–15 and Luton Town 10–2 in the Regional League Midland Division match of 1939–40. In the Football League Coventry beat Bristol City 9–0 in 1933–34.

GOALS – CAREER BEST

The highest goal scorer in the club's history is Clarrie Bourton, who between season 1931–32 and the end of season 1936–37 had netted 181 goals for the Sky Blues. These comprised of 172 league goals and nine FA Cup goals.

GOALS – INDIVIDUAL

The most goals scored by a Coventry City player in any one match is five by Clarrie Bourton, Arthur Bacon and Cyrille Regis.

Clarrie Bourton was the first to achieve the feat in a 6–1 home win over Bournemouth on 17 October 1931. Arthur Bacon netted five goals two seasons later as City beat Gillingham 7–3 at the Priestfield Stadium in a Third Division (South) match on 30 December 1933. The last Coventry player to score five goals in a match was Cyrille Regis in City's 7–2 home League Cup victory over Chester City on 9 October 1985.

GOALS – SEASON

The club's highest league goal-scorer in any one season remains Clarrie Bourton who scored forty nine league goals in 1931–32 as City finished twelfth in the Third Division (South). He also scored when the Highfield Road club drew 2–2 with Clapton Orient in the first round of the FA Cup. He scored five goals in City's 6–1 victory over Bournemouth, four in the 5–1 win over Mansfield Town and hat-tricks against Clapton Orient (Home 4–2) Reading (Home 5–1) Crystal Palace (Home 8–0) Mansfield Town (Away 3–3) and Watford (Home 5–0).

GOULD, BOBBY

A much-travelled striker and great hearted competitor, Bobby Gould

Bobby Gould.

began his career with his home club, Coventry City. He made his debut at the age of seventeen in a goal-less draw at Shrewsbury Town in October 1963 but over the next three seasons he only made twenty nine League and Cup appearances.

He won a regular place in the City side in 1966–67, top-scoring with twenty four goals in thirty nine games as the club won the Second Division Championship. Included in that total was a hat-trick in a 5–0 home win over Ipswich Town.

In what was the club's first season in the top flight, Gould suffered a number of injuries, only playing in fourteen games. He still managed to score eight goals including a hat-trick in a 5–1 defeat of Burnley. He

56

had scored forty two goals in eighty nine games when he moved to Arsenal where he was a member of the Gunners' side that lost to Third Division Swindon Town in the League Cup Final of 1969.

He joined Wolves in the summer of 1970 and ended his first season with the Molineux club as their leading scorer with twenty four goals including a hat-trick against Manchester United. Early the following season he joined West Bromwich Albion, scoring eighteen goals in fifty two games before signing for Bristol City. In November 1973 he moved to West Ham United and was instrumental in the club reaching the FA Cup Final the following season. Gould then rejoined Wolves, taking his tally of goals to thirty nine in ninety three games in his two spells with that club.

He later became manager at Eastville before being appointed Coventry manager in May 1983. With the majority of senior players wanting to leave Highfield Road, Gould had to rebuild the team. In eighteen months in the job he brought in twenty five new players including Peake, Gynn, Pearce, Bennett, Ogrizovic, Kilcline and Regis but with City in twenty first place in the First Division in December 1984, he was sacked. He returned to take over the reins at Bristol Rovers again before leading Wimbledon to their 1988 FA Cup Final success over Liverpool.

He moved back to Highfield Road in 1992 after an unhappy spell in charge of West Bromwich Albion. He later became Welsh national team manager before resigning in the summer of 1999.

GUEST PLAYERS

The guest system was used by all clubs during the two wars. Although at times it was abused almost beyond belief (ie: some sides that opposed Coventry had ten or eleven guests) it normally worked sensibly and effectively to the benefit of players, clubs and supporters alike.

In the First World War, West Bromwich Albion and England defender Jesse Pennington and Dundee and Scotland international George Chaplin both guested for City and Gil Merrick, the Birmingham City and England goalkeeper, played for the club in World War Two.

57

GYNN, MICKY

Micky Gynn began his Football League career with his home club, Peterborough United, where he scored thirty three goals in 156 league games before signing for Coventry City for £60,000 in the summer of 1983. He played his first game for the club in a 3–2 defeat at Watford on the opening day of the 1983–84 season.

Micky Gynn.

In his early days with City Gynn found himself in and out of the side but came into his own during the Sky Blues' FA Cup run of 1986–87. He scored the only goal of the game against Stoke City in the fifth round and netted the equaliser in the 3–2 semi-final win over Leeds United. In the Cup Final, Gynn replaced the injured Brian Borrows and must have covered every blade of grass on the Wembley pitch. His next two seasons at Highfield Road saw him suffer a number of injury problems but in 1989–90 he returned to full fitness and won a regular place in the side.

He went on to score forty five goals in 295 games for Coventry before hanging up his boots.

H

HATELEY, MARK

This prolific goal scorer with the club's youth and reserve teams finally got his first team chance at Highfield Road against Wolverhampton Wanderers in May 1979. Over the next three seasons he only appeared in thirty four games, scoring two goals, but in 1981–82 he won a regular place and was the club's top scorer with eighteen goals in thirty nine games. His total included his first hat-trick for the club in a 5–5 draw at Southampton. His performances in the Coventry attack led to him winning international recognition and he scored twice on his debut for England Under--21s. Hateley went on to score thirty four goals in 111 games for the Sky Blues before Second Division Portsmouth offered £50,000 for his services. An independent tribunal set the fee at £190,000 – still on the low side for a player of his class.

Mark Hateley.

Within a year of his arrival at Fratton Park Hateley had won the first of his thirty two caps and, in his second game for his country, scored against Brazil in the Maracana Stadium. Hateley only spent one season with Pompey, scoring twenty five goals in forty four games, a total which included hat-tricks against Cambridge United and Grimsby Town in the space of four days.

Hateley joined AC Milan for £1 million, but after three years at the San Siro he moved to Monaco before, in 1990, he joined Glasgow Rangers. After 216 games for the Ibrox club he moved back south to play for Queen's Park Rangers. When he was at Loftus Road he had a loan spell at Leeds United before returning to Ibrox for a second spell. In the summer of 1997 he was selected as the man to bring back the glory days to Boothferry Park, joining Hull City as player/manager.

HAT-TRICKS

One of the club's earliest hat-trick heroes was Billy Smith who in 1907–08 scored thirty three goals in thrity three Southern League games including hat-tricks against Stourbridge (Away 9–1)and Stoke Reserves (Home 5–0); four goals against Brierley Hill (Home 6–0); and five against West Bromwich Albion Reserves (Home 11–2). Unbelievably, at the end of the season City forgot to re-sign him and he joined Small Heath before returning to Highfield Road a year later.

During the 1958–59 season, Jimmy Rogers scored four goals in the 7–1 home win over Aldershot and then nine days later netted a hat-trick in the return match at the Recreation Ground which City won 4–1.

One of the best performances in recent years came in 1977–78 when Mick Ferguson netted three hat-tricks in the wins over Manchester City (Home 4–2), Wolves (Away 3–1) and Birmingham City (Home 4–0).

On 10 December 1983, Terry Gibson scored a hat-trick for Coventry in a 4–0 win over Liverpool at Highfield Road. It was the first hat-trick scored against Liverpool since Keith Weller did so for Leicester City in a 3–2 win in August 1972.

HERBERT, FRANK

Frank 'Cute' Herbert played his early football with Foxford United in the Coventry and Warwickshire League and in one of his three seasons with the club scored more than 100 goals. After a spell with Bedworth United, he joined Exhall Colliery from where Coventry manager Albert Evans signed him in 1922.

He made his debut in November of that year in a 5–1 defeat at Stockport County. It was the following season before he established himself as a first team regular, operating at either inside or outside-left. He became one of the club's most popular players, his best season in terms of goals scored being in 1926–27 when he netted twenty six goals in forty one games. He had scored his first hat-trick for City the previous season in a 7–1 home win over Rotherham United. During that 1926–27 season his total included four goals in a 5–1 home win over Watford on New Year's Day as he ended the campaign as the club's leading goal scorer. Herbert continued. to score goals for the Highfield Road club until he retired in 1929, finishing his Coventry career with eighty eight goals in 200 games.

HIGHFIELD ROAD

Highfield Road opened on 9 September 1899 with a new 2,000 seat stand on the south side of the ground. The new ground cost £60 a year to rent but the club were helped out by sub-letting the pitch to Clifton Victoria, a local junior team. After the club's decent FA Cup run in 1910, a new stand with a barrel roof was built on the north side of the ground. Three years after Coventry had been admitted to the Football League, the Kop was built up from waste rubble left over from the building of the city's tram track. In 1927 the West Terrace was covered by a roof bought from Twickenham at a cost of £2,200. Following the club's promotion back to the Second Division, the original stand of 1899 was demolished to make way for a new Main Stand costing £14,000. Also in 1936, the club purchased the freehold of the ground for £20,000, thanks to a loan from the chairman of Armstrong-Siddeley, one of a number of Coventry-based motor manufacturing companies. Two years later, additional terracing was added to the Kop and was known as the Crow's Nest. In 1939 the roof of the Main Stand was extended to cover the paddock.

During the 'Coventry blitz' air raids of November 1940 the ground was hit three times but the only real damage was to the playing area.

Floodlights were first installed in October 1953 and first used for a friendly game against Queen of the South. Four years later an improved set of lights replaced the original ones and were first switched on for the visit of Third Lanark. In 1963, following the arrival of Jimmy Hill, the Thackhall Street Stand on the north side of the ground was replaced by the Sky Blues Stand at a cost of £120,000. The following year the Coventry Evening Telegraph sponsored a new £3,000 electronic scoreboard positioned at the rear of the Kop.

When the club was promoted to the First Division in 1967 the double decker West Stand was built at a cost of £85,000. That season had seen Highfield Road house its largest crowd when 51,455 saw the Second Division Championship decider against Wolves. On 16 March 1968, the club's Main Stand was gutted by fire. Almost immediately City rebuilt it at a cost of £150,000.

In 1973 defects were discovered in the roof of the Sky Blue Stand that necessitated the replacement of the vaulted section with a flat roof. Eight years later Highfield Road became the first all-seater stadium in England when 8,000 extra seats were installed, thus reducing the ground's capacity to 20,600. Two years later, with attendances dropping at an alarming rate, the Kop above the seating area was reopened as a standing terrace and in 1985 all the seats were removed.

Following the Taylor Report, a new East Stand was built in 1994, a year which also saw the Sky Blues Stand roof replaced by a much deeper one. The cost of these alterations was £4.3 million. In 1995 all the ground's pre-1990 seats were replaced and the executive boxes on the Main Stand paddock removed. Later the original vaulted roof of the Main Stand was replaced by one with goal posts style supports, bringing the post-Taylor Report expenditure to £7 million.

HILL, BRIAN

Although he was the club's youngest debutant and goal scorer at the age of 16 years 273 days in a 3–2 defeat at Gillingham on the final day of the 1957–58 campaign, it was another five seasons before Brian Hill established himself as a first team regular. He appeared in the Sky Blues side in fourteen seasons of league football and showed his versatility by playing in all ten different numbered outfield shirts.

He helped the club win the Third Division Championship in 1963–64 and the Second Division title in 1966–67. In a career that was littered with niggling injuries Hill played in 281 League and Cup games before, following a loan spell at Bristol City, he joined Torquay United. His stay at Plainmoor was brief and he soon returned to the West Midlands to play non-league football for Bedworth United.

HILL, JIMMY

Jimmy Hill's enthusiasm for the game of football as led to him being a player, union leader, manager, director, television personality and even an emergency linesman. He was first spotted by Reading manager Ted Drake playing for his regiment when on National Service, and turned out as an amateur for the then Elm Park club. After not being offered terms he moved to Brentford as a professional before later playing for Fulham. He spent the rest of his playing career at Craven Cottage until a knee injury brought his playing career to a close in 1961.

In 1956, Hill had become chairman of the Professional Footballers' Association and shot to prominence when he fought to rid the game of the restrictive £20 a week maximum wage.

In November 1961 Jimmy Hill joined Coventry City as manager. He soon instilled confidence into those around him and made the City players better performers than they actually were. In 1963–64 he led the club to the Third Division Championship and the Second Division title followed three years later. These were great times at Highfield Road as the 'Sky Blue Revolution' was met with a great increase in attendances. Hill left Coventry in September 1968 after receiving a lucrative offer to become head of sport with London Weekend Television. The move stunned the City fans, many of whom believed Hill had left because the team was not strong enough to survive in the top flight.

A qualified FA coach and referee, he once made an appearance as an emergency linesman at Arsenal when the original linesman was injured. Hill was working for television that day at Highbury and when a call was made for a replacement he took up the challenge.

In October 1972 he left London Weekend Television to set up his own television consultancy group and became commercial manager at Fulham. He returned to Coventry as managing director in April 1975 and later, as chairman of the club, incurred the fans' wrath when he made Highfield Road an all-seater stadium. He had to back down and allow terraces to be reintroduced though the Taylor Report showed that perhaps he was right. On leaving Coventry at the end of the 1982–83 season Hill became director of Charlton Athletic where he was involved in the decision which removed the club from The Valley to Selhurst Park in 1985. He left Charlton in 1987 to become chairman of Fulham, a position he held until 1997.

HILL, PETER

After joining Coventry from Modern Machines FC in 1946 Peter Hill made his first team debut in a 2–1 defeat at Sheffield Wednesday in February 1949. Over the next three seasons he made just nine league appearances before establishing himself as a first team regular in 1952–53. In only his third game of that campaign he scored his first hat-trick for the club in a 3–0 home win over Leyton Orient and ended the season with thirteen League and Cup goals – his best return in fourteen seasons in the Coventry side. In those days, Hill played at inside-forward and continued to score on a regular basis, netting his second hat-trick for the club in March 1958 as Aldershot were beaten 6–0 at Highfield Road.

During the early part of the club's promotion-winning season of 1958–59 he switched to playing wide on the right wing and although he provided most of the crosses from which Ray Straw scored his goals, he still managed his fair share including his sensational strike against Norwich City in April 1960.

He went on to score seventy seven goals in 303 League and Cup games before retiring to become the club's trainer. He held that position for five years before leaving to work in local industry. He returned to Highfield Road in 1988 as the club's kit manager.

HOLTON, JIM

Jim Holton was one of Manchester United manager Tommy Docherty's first signings when he paid Shrewsbury Town £80,000 for his services in 1973. Holton was a giant of a centre-half and a great favourite at United as they won the Second Division Championship. 'Six foot two, eyes of blue, Big Jim Holton's after you!' sang the Stretford End. However, in

December 1975 he broke a leg and never played first team football again for the club. He was playing for the reserves when he tragically broke his leg again. It marked the end of his United days and he was transferred to Sunderland. Holton was a determined character and despite his injuries he clawed his way back to fitness with the Wearsiders. However, just six months after arriving at Roker Park he was on his way to Coventry City and made his debut in a 1–1 home draw against West Bromwich Albion. When he arrived at Highfield Road the club was languishing near the foot of the First Division but two wins and four draws in his eight appearances helped it remain in the top flight.

Holton, who won fifteen caps for Scotland, stayed with the Sky Blues until 1982 when, after making 100 League and Cup appearances, he joined Sheffield Wednesday. His only goal for Coventry came in a 2–0 win at Huddersfield Town in the 1977–78 League Cup competition. On his retirement he ran the Old Stag pub in Coventry until his sudden death in 1993.

HOME MATCHES

Coventry's best home wins in the league is the 9–0 rout of Bristol City in a Third Division (South) match on 28 April 1934. The Sky Blues have also scored eight goals in a match on three occasions, beating Crystal Palace 8–0 in 1931–32 and 8–1 in 1935–36 and Shrewsbury Town 8–1 in 1963–64. The club's biggest home win in the FA Cup is the 7–0 defeat of Scunthorpe United in a first round tie on 24 November 1934.

HOME SEASONS

Coventry City have never gone through a complete league season with an undefeated home record but did lose just one home match in seasons 1935–36, 1946–47, 1958–59 and 1966–67. The club's highest number of home wins in a league season is nineteen. This was achieved in 1935–36 from twenty one matches as the club won the Third Division (South) Championship.

HOUCHEN, KEITH

Middlesbrough–born striker Keith Houchen began his league career with Hartlepool United, scoring sixty five goals in 170 league games before joining Leyton Orient. In two years at Brisbane Road, Houchen scored twenty goals in seventy six games before moving to York City in March 1984. With the Bootham Crescent club he scored the goal that knocked Arsenal out of the FA Cup. Towards the end of the 1985–86 season, Houchen, who had scored nineteen goals in sixty seven games for the Minstermen, joined Scunthorpe United. His stay with the Ironsides was brief and in the summer of 1986 he signed for Coventry for £60,000.

He made his debut for the Sky Blues in a 1–0 defeat at West Ham United on the opening day of the 1986–87 season and though his performances in the league side were poor, he scored some vital goals in the club's FA Cup run. He netted five goals in five games including the winner at Manchester United, two in the 3–1 sixth round win at Sheffield Wednesday, one in the 3–2 semi-final defeat of Leeds United and the diving header in the final against Spurs, which saw Coventry win the FA Cup, beating the White Hart Lane club 3–2.

Despite these performances, Houchen was never able to establish himself in the Coventry side and after scoring twelve goals in sixty five games he joined Hibernians for £300,000. Following similar scoring problems with the Easter Road club he moved to Port Vale before later returning to Hartlepool United as player/coach and then the player/manager.

HOWE, DON

Don Howe began his career at the Hawthorns and, in twelve years with West Bromwich Albion, played in nearly 400 games scoring nineteen goals, mainly from the penalty spot. With the Baggies he won twenty three England caps and played in the 1958 World Cup tournament. In April 1964, he was transferred to Arsenal for £40,000, then a record fee for a full-back. He was soon made club captain at Highbury but in a game against Blackpool in March 1966 he broke his leg. The injury forced his retirement from league football alhough he stayed at Highbury as first team coach. Recognised as the driving force behind the Gunners' side that won the League and Cup double in 1971, he was appointed West Bromwich Albion manager two months later.

He was not too successful in his period in charge at the Hawthorns and they were relegated in 1973. After two unsuccessful seasons in the lower divisions Howe resigned his post. Subsequently he coached Galatasaray; Leeds United; Arsenal – where he also spent two years as manager; Bristol Rovers; and Wimbledon when the Dons won the FA Cup in 1988. After a spell at Queen's Park Rangers he replaced Terry Butcher as manager of Coventry City.

Howe was reluctant to take over but after being joined by Bobby Gould, accepted an eighteen month contract. However, in July 1992 after six months in charge, Howe decided to accept an offer to become Chelsea's assistant-manager to Ian Porterfield. He had been suffering from heart problems but on leaving Stamford Bridge was appointed technical coaching advisor in the England set-up.

HUCKERBY, DARREN

Darren Huckerby's performances for Lincoln City led to a number of top flight clubs making offers for the Nottingham-born youngster. It was Newcastle United who secured his signature when they paid £400,000 for him in November 1995. Following two appearances as a substitute he had a loan period at Millwall before joining Coventry City for £1 million in November 1996.

He made his debut for the Sky Blues as a substitute in a 2–1 home defeat by Aston Villa before, three games later, scoring his first Coventry goal against Newcastle United, the club that had sold him a few weeks earlier. That season he scored seven goals in twenty nine games, his form leading to him being selected for the England Under-21 side. In 1997–98 his first full season, he was nominated for the PFA's Young Player of the Year and played for England 'B' against Chile. He scored fourteen goals including a hat-trick in a 3–3 draw at Leeds United.

The scorer of a number of spectacular goals, Huckerby netted another hat-trick in 1998–99 as Nottingham Forest were beaten 4–0 to take his tally of goals to thirty one in 103 games. However, after just two games of the 1999–2000 season, he was sold to Leeds United for £5.5 million.

HUDSON, GEORGE

George Hudson began his career with Blackburn Rovers before leaving to play for Accrington Stanley, where he scored thirty five goals in forty four league games. He left Peel Park in October 1961 to join Peterborough United where he continued to score on a regular basis, netting thirty nine in sixty five games.

In April 1963 Jimmy Hill paid a club record fee of £21,000 to take him to Highfield Road and he responded by scoring a hat-trick on his debut in a 5–4 win over Halifax Town. The following season Coventry won the Third Division Championship and Hudson was the top scorer with twenty four league goals. His total included a hat-trick in the 6–3 win at Queen's Park Rangers and the Manchester-born striker also netted another treble in the 6–1 FA Cup win at Trowbridge. Hudson top-scored again in 1964–65 with twenty four goals in forty three League and Cup games, netting a hat-trick in the final game of the season as City won 3–1 at Leyton Orient. Hudson went on to score seventy five goals in 129 games before being sold to Northampton Town for £22,000.

Within twelve months of his move to the County Ground, Hudson had left and joined Tranmere Rovers, helping the Prenton Park club to promotion to the Third Division in his first season on the Wirral. He scored a hat-trick in a 5–1 FA Cup win over Rochdale in December 1967 but at the end of the following season, after having scored twenty two goals in sixty four games, he left first class football.

HUMPHRIES, WILLIE

At school Willie Humphries was a rugby scrum-half but also shone as a soccer player and joined Glentoran as an amateur when he was working as a clerical officer with the Belfast Transport department. His career took off when he joined Ards and Leeds United beat Blackpool to his signature in September 1958. He failed to settle at Elland Road and returned to Ards in November 1959.

It was Coventry City manager, Jimmy Hill, who persuaded Humphries to have another attempt playing in the Football League and he made his debut for the club in a 2–0 home defeat by Hull City in April 1962. The following season he scored ten goals in fifty one games, his form winning him a recall to the Northern Ireland side for whom he won four caps. In 1963–64 Humphries had an outstanding season as the Sky Blues won the Third Division Championship. In March 1965 after scoring twenty four goals in 126 games he joined Swansea for £14,000.

Although he was unable to keep the Welsh club in the Second Division, he had three good seasons at the Vetch Field, scoring twenty two goals in 143 games before returning to Ireland for his third and longest spell with Ards. During those years he was Footballer of the Year for the Irish League and his side won the cup. Humphries later managed Bangor from 1983 to 1985 before buying a newsagent's business which he ran until he retired in 1991.

HUNDRED GOALS

Coventry City have scored more than 100 league goals in a season on four occasions. The highest total is 108 goals, scored in 1931–32 when they finished twelfth in the Third Division (South). The Sky Blues scored 106 goals the following season when finishing sixth and 100 goals in 1933–34 when they ended the campaign as runners-up in the Third Division (South). The last occasion when Coventry scored more than 100 league goals was 1935–36 when they netted 102 goals in winning the Third Division (South) Championship.

HUNT, ERNIE

Ernie Hunt was working for British Rail when Swindon Town manager Bert Head signed him as an amateur in 1957. With the Wiltshire club Hunt, whose real first name is Roger, won three England Under-23 caps and scored eighty two goals in 214 league games before signing for Wolves in September 1965.

He should have made his debut at Southampton but he decided that he was not fully match fit and watched from the stands as the Saints won 9–3. The following season he helped Wolves win promotion to the First Division, top-scoring with twenty goals in thirty seven games including a hat-trick in a 4–0 win at Northampton Town. Hunt, who had an excellent scoring record for a midfielder, had found the net thirty five times in eighty two outings for Wolves before joining Everton for £80,000.

Unable to settle at Goodison Park, he signed for Coventry City and made his debut in a 2–0 home win over Manchester United in March 1968. At Highfield Road he teamed up with Willie Carr. The two of them perfected the infamous 'donkey kick' which resulted in a spectacular goal on *Match of the Day* as City beat League Champions Everton 3–1. Hunt scored fifty one goals in 123 League and Cup games for the Sky Blues before, following a loan spell with Doncaster Rovers, he ended his career with Bristol City.

HUNT, STEVE

Born at Witton, mid-fielder Steve Hunt made his Football League debut for Aston Villa at Sheffield Wednesday in 1975 but unable to win a place in the side on a regular basis, he left the club to play for New York Cosmos in the NASL for £50,000.

He helped Cosmos win the NASL Championships in 1977 and again in 1978, but in September of that year he returned to these shores, signing for Coventry City for £40,000.

He made his debut for the Sky Blues at Derby County, scoring the opening goal in a 2–0 win. His best season for Coventry in terms of goals scored was 1981–82 when he netted twelve in forty one games, but in March 1984, after scoring thirty four goals in 216 League and Cup games, he joined West Bromwich Albion for £80,000.

He won two caps for England when with the Baggies, However, when Ron Saunders arrived to manage Albion Hunt's face did not fit and he rejoined Villa in a deal involving Darren Bradley plus £90,000. Hunt was a regular in the Villa side until the appointment of Graham Taylor, after which his appearances were restricted. In November 1987 injury forced his retirement from the game.

Steve Hunt.

HUTCHISON, TOMMY

One of the most naturally gifted players of the post-war era, Scottish international Tommy Hutchison began his career with Alloa before Blackpool brought him into League football in 1968.

In 1969–70 he helped the Seasiders win promotion to the First Division, laying on countless chances for his team mates. However, success was short-lived and Blackpool were relegated after just one season in the top flight. Hutchison continued to impress with his close control, pinpoint crosses and ability to beat a player with skill and pace and it came as no surprise when he joined Coventry City in October 1972.

He made his debut for the Sky Blues in a 3–2 home win over Manchester City and in the next eight seasons scored thirty goals in 355 games. During that time he helped to transform the club into one of the most attractive outfits in the top flight.

In 1973 he won the first of seventeen full Scottish caps, all while at Highfield Road. On leaving Coventry, he joined Manchester City, proving to be one of John Bond's most influential signings. He helped the Maine Road club to a League Cup semi-final and the FA Cup Final where he had the misfortune to score a late equaliser for Spurs when he deflected Glenn Hoddle's shot past Joe Corrigan. On leaving Maine Road he spent a season in Hong Kong before joining Burnley. Never fully accepted by the Turf Moor crowd, he moved on to Swansea in July 1985.

He later became player/coach at the Vetch Field and helped them win promotion to the First Division in 1987–88. In 1988–89 he was virtually an ever-present and competed in the European Cup Winners' Cup in 1989–90 at the age of forty two – the oldest player ever to play in a European tie. On his retirement he received a PFA Merit Award for his services to football after 860 league appearances for his five clubs.

The popular Scot then became Football in the Community Officer at Merthyr Tydfil, passing on his vast knowledge of the game at coaching sessions throughout South Wales.

I

INJURIES

The risk of serious injury is an ever-present threat in the game of football and all professional players expect to miss games through injury at some point in their careers. Perhaps the most tragic injury in recent years befell David Busst who suffered a compound fracture of his right leg at Old Trafford on East Monday 1996 and has sadly not played league football since.

One of the most unusual injuries occurred to City goalkeeper Jim Blyth who injured his back when warming up before the home game against Norwich City on 1 September 1979 and had to be replaced before kick-off by Steve Murcott.

INTER CITIES FAIRS CUP

Although they beat Spurs in the 1987 FA Cup Final the Sky Blues were robbed of the opportunity to play in Europe because of the ban imposed on English teams following the Heysel disaster. The club's only European campaign was in the 1970–71 Inter Cities Fairs Cup, the last season before it was changed to the UEFA Cup.

During the club's first game away to Bulgarian side, Trakin Plovdiv, City manager Noel Cantwell adopted a counter-attacking strategy with which the Bulgarians could not cope. Two goals from O'Rourke and Martin just before half-time left Plovdiv deflated. John O'Rourke claimed his second and Coventry's third in the 66th minute and although the home side pulled a goal back, O'Rourke completed his hat-trick with two minutes of the game remaining. In the second leg both Joicey and Blockley scored within the first five minutes. The crowd were expecting a goal feast but there was no further scoring and the Sky Blues progressed to the second round by an aggregate score of 6–1.

The club's opponents were Bayern Munich. Ernie Hunt equalised for Coventry after the Germans had taken a first-minute lead on home soil,

Bayern stepped up a gear and after nineteen minutes were 4–1 up. Two second half goals left Coventry with a mountain to climb in the return match at Highfield Road. However, the Sky Blues regained much pride with a 2–1 victory, thanks to goals by Martin and O'Rourke.

INTERNATIONAL PLAYERS

Coventry City's most capped players (ie: caps gained while players were registered with the club) are Ronnie Rees and Dave Clements with twenty one apiece. The following is a complete list of players who have gained full international honours:

England		Scotland	
Dion Dublin	3	Jim Blyth	2
Reg Matthews	5	Willie Carr	6
Cyrille Regis	1	Kevin Gallacher	1
Danny Thomas	2	Tommy Hutchison	17
Northern Ireland		Eion Jess	3
Hugh Bare	2	Gary McAllister	12
Jackie Brown	4	David Speedie	5
Dave Clements	21	Colin Stein	4
Willie Humphries	10	Ian Wallace	3
Norman Lockhart	3	**Wales**	
Michael O'Neill	2	Bryn Allen	2
Republic of Ireland		Les Cartwright	5
Phil Babb	9	Bob Evans	5
Gary Breen	6	Simon Haworth	4
Jackie Brown	2	Leslie Jones	5
Liam Daish	3	George Lowrie	3
Gerry Daly	15	Don Nardiello	2
Ashley Grimes	2	David Phillips	9
Jimmy Holmes	17	Ronnie Rees	21
		Terry Yorath	20

The first Coventry City player to be capped was Bob Evans who played for Wales v Ireland in 1911.

J

JONES, LESLIE

Inside-forward Leslie Jones began his career with his home club, Aberdare Athletic, before joining Cardiff City in 1929. He soon struck up a formidable left-wing pertnership with Walter Robbins and in the next five seasons he played in 161 League and Cup games, with his most prolific season being 1932–33 when he scored sixteen goals. His performances during that campaign led to him winning the first of eleven Welsh caps when he played against France.

His all-action displays in the Christmas matches of 1933 persuaded Coventry City manager Harry Storer to pay £2,000 for his services. He made his debut in a 4–1 defeat at Bristol Rovers but by the end of the season he had scored ten goals in sixteen games, including a hat-trick in a 4–1 home win over Bournemouth as Coventry finished as runners-up in the Third Division (South). In 1934–35 he topped the club's goal scoring charts with thirty goals in forty four games as Coventry ended the campaign in third place. Included in his total were hat-tricks against Clapton Orient (Home 4–0) Southend United (Home 6–3) Gillingham (Away 5–2) and Newport County (Home 5–0). In 1935–36 he won a Third Division (South) League Championship medal, his twenty goals including a hat-trick in a 6–1 win over Queen's Park Rangers. Coventry resisted a £7,000 bid from Tottenham but could not refuse Arsenal's offer in 1937 and, after scoring seventy four goals in 144 games, Jones moved to Highbury.

He helped the Gunners win the League Championship in 1937–38 and in the last season before the Second World War he won an FA Charity Shield winners' medal against Preston North End.

During the hostilities he continued to play for the Highbury club and won five war-time caps. On the return of peace he was granted a free transfer and moved to Swansea Town as player/coach. His stay at Vetch

Field was short-lived and he became player/manager of Barry Town, before returning to League football with Brighton. He later managed Scunthorpe United.

JUBILEE FUND

The League Benevolent Fund was launched in 1938, fifty years after the start of the Football League, to help players who had fallen on hard times. It was decided that the best way to raise funds was for sides to play local derby games without taking into account league status.

Just before the start of the 1938–39 season City beat Birmingham 2–0 at Highfield Road in the Jubilee Fund game and then won again 3–2 prior to the start of the 1939–40 campaign.

K

KEARNS, MICK

Nuneaton-born Mick Kearns could play at either full-back or wing-half and, despite playing in a mediocre Coventry side in the early 1960s, was unlucky not to win international recognition. He played his first game for the club in a 3–0 home defeat by Bournemouth in September 1957 but only made three appearances that season as the Sky Blues finished nineteenth in the Third Division (South).

Following reorganisation Coventry found themselves in the Fourth Division for the 1958–59 season but Kearns, who played in thirty two games, helped them win promotion at the first attempt.

Despite being plagued by a knee injury throughout most of his career he missed very few games in his ten seasons in the first team. In 1962–63 he played in all of the club's nine FA Cup games as it reached the sixth round before losing to Manchester United. The following season he played his part as Coventry won the Third Division Championship and, after three seasons in the Second Division, finally won promotion to the top flight as that division's champions.

Kearns was a regular member of the Sky Blues' side during the first half of the club's inaugural season in Division One but injuries began to take their toll and at the end of that campaign, after which he had scored sixteen goals in 382 games, he hung up his boots.

He later returned to the game as a member of Coventry's coaching staff, later becoming the club's chief scout.

KERR, JAMES

Born in Annan, Scotland in November 1881, James Kerr spent a long time at Bathgate FC before being appointed manager of Coventry City. Although he never had any great success with the Highfield Road club he always produced entertaining sides. During his three seasons in charge,

City finished sixteenth in 1925–26, fifteenth in 1926–27 and twentieth in 1927–28, by which time he had been sacked. Kerr moved the short distance to Fellows Park to become manager of Walsall but in just one season in charge he met with little success.

In April 1929 he became manager of Norwich City and in his first season he led the club to eighth place in the Third Division (South), their best season since joining the League. However, the following season, the Canaries finished bottom of the table.

Kerr entered hospital with pneumonia in January 1933 and sadly died the following month. It came as a great shock for he had never had a serious illness before.

KILCLINE, BRIAN

The first Coventry City captain to hold aloft the FA Cup when the Sky Blues beat Tottenham Hotspur 3–2 in 1987, Brian Kilcline began his league career with Notts County. In four seasons with the Meadow Lane club, he made 184 first team appearances and won international recognition at England Under-21 level before joining Coventry in the summer of 1984 for £60,000.

He made his debut for the Sky Blues in a 1–0 defeat at Aston Villa on the opening day of the 1984–85 season, going on to score two goals in twenty six games, including the only goal of the game against Luton Town which assured the that club would play top flight football the following season. Kilcline was to score several vital goals, usually with his head or from the penalty spot, where he missed very few until the 1989–90 season.

An inspirational captain, he formed an outstanding central defensive partnership with Trevor Peake and went on to score thirty five goals in 211 games before leaving Highfield Road to join Oldham Athletic for £400,000.

Brian Kilcline.

77

During his seven seasons with Coventry he suffered a series of niggling injuries which sadly reduced his number of appearances for the club.

His stay with Oldham was brief and in February he signed for Newcastle United for £250,000. Injuries blighted his career at St James Park and in a little under two years with the Magpies he only made forty five first team appearances. In January 1994 he was on the move again, this time to Swindon Town, before joining Mansfield Town where he played some of the best football of his long career before parting company at the end of the 1997–98 season.

KIRK, ROY

After being blooded in the Yorkshire Midweek League Roy Kirk continued his early football career with Bolsover Colliery, where he played at centre-forward, centre-half, right-half and outside-right. He joined Leeds United in October 1948 as understudy to the great John Charles but in almost four years at Elland Road he only made thirty nine appearances.

In March 1952, Coventry paid £10,000 to take him to Highfield Road and he made his debut in a 3–1 defeat at Nottingham Forest. Kirk had been bought to replace George Mason, and over the next ten seasons gave the club great service. He was ever-present in seasons 1953–54, 1954–55 and 1958–59 when the club won promotion from the Fourth Division. This season saw Kirk move to play at right-back following the emergence of centre-half George Curtis.

Kirk went on to play in 345 League and Cup games for City and although he only scored seven goals, the one he scored in the club's 1–0 FA Cup win over Northampton Town on 20 November 1954 was remarkable. Standing in his own penalty area, the Coventry defender hit the ball fully 80 yards over the head of former City 'keeper, Alf Wood, into the Northampton goal.

He left Highfield Road in 1960 to play Southern League football for Cambridge United. He later became manager and helped lay the foundations of the club which Bill Leivers got into the Football League. Kirk became Cambridge City's manager in 1967.

L

LAKE, BILLY

He began his Football League career with Walsall where his father was on the board of directors. He spent just one season, 1927–28 at Fellows Park before leaving to join Coventry. Lake made his City debut in a 3–1 defeat at Queen's Park Rangers in December 1928 and in the following season he won a regular place in the side.

During the 1929–30 season he formed a fine partnership with Jimmy Loughlin, scoring fifteen goals including a hat-trick in a 3–1 home win over Norwich City. Lake was the club's top scorer in 1930–31, his total of twenty four goals including four in a 5–1 home defeat of Bristol Rovers. From 1931–32 onwards Billy Lake was overshadowed by the prolific goal scoring talents of Clarrie Bourton. However, he too continued to find the net, scoring hat-tricks against Fulham (Home 5–5) on 2 January 1932 and Queen's Park Rangers (Home 7–0) on 4 March 1933. Following the signing of Leslie Jones, Lake's appearances were restricted, although when he did play he showed that he had not lost his touch. When Coventry entertained Luton Town in February 1938, Lake scored all four goals in a 4–1 win over the Hatters.

Lake, who had scored 123 goals in 295 League and Cup games decided to retire once war had been declared.

LARGEST CROWD

It was on 29 April 1967 that Highfield Road housed its largest crowd. The occasion was a Second Division promotion match against Wolverhampton Wanderers. A staggering large crowd of 51,455 saw the Sky Blues win 3–1 with goals from Machin, Gibson and Rees. The club was unbeaten in its final two matches and won the Second Division Championship, finishing one point ahead of Wolves, who were the runners-up.

LATE FINISHES

Coventry's final match of the season against Chesterfield at Saltergate on 26 May 1947 is the latest date for the finish of any Sky Blue's season. During the Second World War many curious things occurred, among them the continuance of the 1939–40 season into June. Thus, City's last competitive match in that campaign was on 8 June when a Murray hat-trick helped the club beat West Bromwich Albion 4–0 in a Regional League Midland Division match.

LAUDERDALE, JOCK

Jock Lauderdale played for both Third Lanark and Queen of the South before coming south of the border to play for Blackpool. He had scored just six goals in twenty one games for the Seasiders when Coventry manager Harry Storer paid £270 for his services in the summer of 1931.

He scored on his debut in a 5–3 defeat at Fulham on the opening day of the 1931–32 season. Partnering Clarrie Bourton up front Lauderdale, who was ever-present, scored nineteen goals including netting in five consecutive games towards the end of the season. Lauderdale was a regular member of the Coventry side for five seasons, scoring sixty three goals in 182 League and Cup games before leaving to play for Northampton Town for £1,700.

A loss of form hampered his progress with the Cobblers and at the end of the 1938–39 season he left to play non-league football for Nuneaton Borough. However, during the war years, he made five guest appearances for the Highfield Road club before finally hanging up his boots.

LEADING GOAL SCORERS

Coventry City have provided the Football League's divisional leading goalscorer on four occasions. They are:

1931–32	Clarrie Bourton	Third Division (South)	49 goals
1932–33	Clarrie Bourton	Third Division (South)	40 goals
1962–63	George Hudson	Third Division	30 goals
1966–67	Bobby Gould	Second Division	24 goals

LEAGUE GOALS – CAREER HIGHEST

Clarrie Bourton holds the Highfield Road record for the most league goals with a career total of 171 goals between 1931–32 and 1936–37.

LEAGUE GOALS – LEAST CONCEDED

During the 1970–71 season, the Sky Blues conceded just 38 goals in 42 games when finishing 10th in the First Division.

LEAGUE GOALS – MOST INDIVIDUAL

Clarrie Bourton holds the Coventry City record for the most league goals in a season with the forty nine he scored in 1931–32 when the club finished twelfth in the Third Division (South).

LEAGUE GOALS – MOST SCORED

Coventry's highest goals tally in the Football League was during the Third Division (South) campaign of 1931–32 when they scored 108 goals.

LEAGUE VICTORY – HIGHEST

City's best league victory is the 9–0 win over Bristol City at Highfield Road on 28 April 1934. Clarrie Bourton netted four goals; Leslie Jones and Fred White scored two goals apiece;and Jock Lauderdale scored one. It was a season in which the club went close to promotion from the Third Division (South), finishing as runners-up seven points behind Norwich City in the days when only the champions were promoted.

LIGHTENING, ARTHUR

Durban-born goalkeeper Arthur Lightening was brought over from South Africa by Nottingham Forest in December 1956 but was unable to win a regular place in the City Ground club's side. Two years later he joined Coventry City along with wing-half Ron Farmer in a double deal that cost the Highfield Road club £6,000.

Lightening made his debut in a 4–1 home win over Hartlepool United and went on to appear in the remaining twenty five games in that 1958–59 season as City won promotion to the Third Division. He was ever-present in 1959–60 as the club finished fourth in Division Three, his performances being favourably compared to former 'keeper Reg Matthews. Lightening had played in 160 games for the Highfield Road club when new manager Jimmy Hill inexplicably sold him to Middlesbrough for £11,000.

Lightening spent just one season at Ayresome Park, making fifteen league appearances as the Teeside club finished fourth in Division Two. At the end of the 1962–63 season he returned to South Africa to attend his brother's funeral. He did not return to this country.

LOCKHART, NORMAN

After beginning his career with Irish League club Distillery, Belfast-born Norman Lockhart joined Linfield where he won two Irish Cup winners' medals. In October 1946 he joined Swansea Town but after just one season at Vetch Field, he was transferred to Coventry City for £7,000.

He made his debut in a goal-less home draw against Bury on 11 October 1947 and played in all of the thirty one remaining league games. He was a virtual ever-present over the next five seasons, his pinpoint crosses providing numerous chances for Lowrie, Murphy and Chisholm. His best season for City in terms of goals scored was 1951–52 when he top-scored for the club with seventeen goals.

At Highfield Road Lockhart won three full caps for Northern Ireland. He had scored forty four goals in 189 games for Coventry when soon after the club had been relegated to the Third Division, he was transferred to Aston Villa for £15,500. He scored ten goals in seventy four games for Villa before leaving to join Bury in November 1956 where he ended his league career.

LOUGHLIN, JIMMY

Centre-forward Jimmy Loughlin had made a number of appearances in Newcastle United's League Championship winning side of 1926–27 before leaving St James Park to join West Ham United. Unable to settle at

Upton Park he moved to Coventry City in December 1928 and made his debut the following month in a 3–0 home win over Brighton and Hove Albion. He missed just one game from then until the end of the season and scored eight goals in nineteen games as City finished in mid-table position. In 1929–30 he formed a prolific goal scoring partnership with Billy Lake, the pair of them scoring forty seven goals. Loughlin, who was the club's top-scorer, netted thirty of the goals, his total including eight doubles.

Early the following season he was badly injured and having scored thirty nine goals in sixty five games for the Highfield Road club found his league career at an end. In the summer of 1931 he went to play for the Dublin club, Dolphin, where he later ended his career.

LOWEST

The lowest number of goals scored by Coventry City in a single season is thirty five in 1919–20 when the club finished twentieth in Division Two in what was its first season in the Football League. Its lowest points record in the league also occurred that season when it gained just twenty nine points.

LOWRIE, GEORGE

George Lowrie played his early football with Swansea Town, but after being unable to break into the Vetch Field club's first team he left to join Preston North End. He had only played in four league games for the Lilywhites when City manager Harry Storer paid £1,750 for his services in the summer of 1939.

He made his debut in the club's last game of peace-time football, scoring one of the goals in a 4–2 win over Barnsley. During the Second World War, he guested for Northampton Town and while at the County Ground won the first of nine Welsh wartime caps. He returned to Highfield Road in 1942 and over the next few seasons of wartime football scored forty eight goals in seventy four games, including four goals in the game against Northampton Town (Home 5–0) and Notts County (Home 7–0) and hat-tricks against Leicester City (Home 5–1) and Wolves (home 3–2). Also during the war years he netted a hat-trick for Wales against England at Wembley.

When league football resumed in 1946–47, Lowrie was the club's top scorer with ywenty nine goals in thirty six games. His total included four goals in the 5–1 home win over Sheffield Wednesday and hat-tricks against Newport County (Home 6–0) Swansea Town (Home 3–2) Bury (Home 3–1) and Newport County again in the FA Cup (Home 5–2).

He began the 1947–48 season in great style, scoring all four goals in a 4–1 win over Luton Town on the opening day of the season and a hat-trick in the club's third match as Brentford were beaten 4–1 at Griffin Park. Later in the season he netted another four goals in a 5–0 defeat of Bradford but as First Division scouts flocked to Highfield Road to see his prolific marksmanship, his form dipped and he was rested. He eventually left Coventry after scoring forty seven goals in fifty eight League and Cup games to join Newcastle United for a record fee of £18,500 but he was unable to settle in the north-east and moved to Bristol City. In February 1952 he returned to see out his league career with Coventry but after taking his tally of goals to fifty nine in eighty five games, he left to play non-league football for Lovells Athletic.

M

McALLISTER, GARY

Gary McAllister joined his home team, Motherwell, from Fir Park Boys' Club but after playing in seventy games and winning a Scottish First Division Championship medal in 1984–85, he came south to play for Leicester City who paid £125,000 for his services in August 1985. Easily adjusting to the pace of English top flight football, he still could not prevent the Foxes being relegated at the end of his second season at Filbert Street. Over the next three seasons, he was twice Leicester's leading goal scorer and it came as no surprise when he won his first full cap for Scotland against East Germany in April 1990.

Leeds United, who had just returned to the First Division, paid £1 million to take McAllister to Elland Road. He made an immediate impact in the club's midfield and after helping the Yorkshire side finish fourth in 1990–91, played a major role in it winning the League Championship the following season.

He was a member of the Scotland side that played in the European Championship Finals in Sweden and in 1992–93 took over the captaincy of Leeds United and later Scotland. McAllister scored some wonderful goals for Leeds, but after finding the net forty six times in 295 League and Cup games including a hat-trick against Coventry City in October 1995, he joined the Sky Blues in July 1996 for £3 million.

Despite the club failing to win any of their first five league games McAllister was in outstanding form and soon assumed the captaincy. However, as the season wore on, it was evident that his performances in Euro '96 had left him tired. The Coventry skipper injured his knee early the following season and although he tried to make a comeback he damaged a cruciate ligament and was out for the rest of the season. McAllister went on to score 17 goals in 136 games before leaving to play for Liverpool.

McDONALD, BOBBY

Bobby McDonald began his Football League career with Aston Villa where he won a League Cup winners' medal and helped the club win promotion to the First Division. In August 1976 he moved to Coventry City

for £40,000 and, after making his debut in a 1–0 win at Bristol City in the second round of that season's League Cup, went on to play in 160 consecutive league games. During his four seasons at Highfield Road, left-back McDonald scored some spectacular goals in his total of 180 League and Cup appearances.

In October 1980, Manchester City paid £250,000 for McDonald who, in his first season at Maine Road, helped the club to the League Cup semi-final and FA Cup Final where it lost 3–2 to Spurs in a replay. Two years later, Manchester City were relegated and McDonald joined Oxford United. He spent three and a half years at the Manor Ground, helping the club rise to the First Division. He later played for Leeds United

Bobby McDonald.

before a five game loan spell at Wolves completed his league career. He later played for a number of non-league clubs including VS Rugby, Burton Albion and Nuneaton Borough.

McDONNELL, MARTIN

Martin McDonnell began his career with Everton but on his return to Goodison Park, following active service in Normandy and north-west Europe, he was allowed to leave and joined Southport. After just one season at Haig Avenue he left to play for Birmingham City. After helping the St Andrew's club to win the Second Division Championship in 1947–48 he was transferred to Coventry City in October 1949 for a fee of £10,000.

He played his first game for the club in a 2–1 home win over Cardiff City. His first few games were at right-back but it was not long before he

86

was switched to centre-half. McDonnell was a virtual ever-present in the Highfield Road club's side for the next six seasons, going on to play in 245 games before losing his place to Roy Kirk towards the end of the 1954–55 season.

The Newton-le-Willows born defender was signed by Harry Storer for a third time when he joined Derby County in the summer of 1955. With the Rams he appeared in ninety three league games and won a Third Division Championship medal before leaving to end his league career with Crewe Alexandra.

McGRATH, LLOYD

The tough-tackling midfielder known for his man-to-man marking ability made his first appearance for the Sky Blues in an 8–2 defeat at Southampton in April 1984, the club's biggest defeat since the war. He won a regular place the following season even after his third appearance had seen City lose 6–2 to Chelsea when McGrath played centre-half.

In 1986–87 his form was such that he won international recognition for England at Under-21 level when he played against Denmark. He helped Coventry reach that season's FA Cup Final where he performed an effective marking job on Glenn Hoddle and provided the cross which was deflected by Gary Mabbutt into his own net for the winning goal.

Over the next few seasons serious injuries such as a broken leg, a hairline fracture, fractured cheekbone and dislocated shoulder forced him to miss much of the club's league programme. McGrath went on to score five goals in 258 games for Coventry before, following a spell in Hong Kong, he ended his league career with Portsmouth.

McINTYRE, JAMES

James McIntyre appeared for Walsall, Notts County, Northampton and Reading before joining Coventry in the summer of 1905. Although he only spent one season with the club he was the leading scorer with nineteen goals in twenty four games as City finished eleventh in the Birmingham and District League. His total included four goals against Walsall (Home 5–1) and a hat-trick against Burslem Port Vale Reserves (Home 6–1). On hanging up his boots he went to work in the Humber car factory before spending a season refereeing in the North Warwickshire League. In 1907 he returned to Highfield Road as the club's assistant trainer. Within a matter of months he had become the chief trainer, a position he held for five years before moving to The Dell as Southampton's trainer.

During the First World War he returned to Coventry to work in a munitions factory. In August 1919 he returned to The Dell as the club's manager and a year later Saints entered the Football League, narrowly missing promotion in their first season. In 1921–22 they won the Third Division (South) Championship but two years later he left the club to run a hotel in Scotland.

In June 1928 Coventry managed to persuade him back as manager and after leading the club to eleventh in the Third Division (South) in 1928–29, and a best-ever finish of sixth the following season, he left to manage Fulham. He led the Cottagers to the Southern Section title but he was sacked in February 1934 following a poor run of results.

McPHERSON, KEN

Ken McPherson was a big, bustling centre-forward who began his career playing alongside Tommy Lawton at Notts County. In 1953 he moved to Middlesbrough for a fee of £15,000. He scored fifteen goals in thirty three games during two years at Ayresome Park but could not win a regular first team place because of the fine form of Wilf Mannion and Charlie Wayman.

In November 1955 he joined Coventry City for £7,000 and scored on his debut the following month in a 3–0 home win over Newport County. He only played in twenty five league games that season but was the joint top scorer with eighteen goals as Coventry finished eighth in the Third Division (South). The following season he was the club's leading scorer with twenty two goals, a total which included a hat-trick in a 4–2 home win over Bournemouth. The club turned to new signing, Ray Straw, in 1957–58 and at the end of that season McPherson, who had scored forty goals in ninety one games was allowed to join Newport County.

He proved to be a prolific goal scorer for the Somerton Park club, netting fifty one goals in 128 league games before leaving to end his league career with Swindon Town where he was converted to a centre-half.

MACHIN, ERNIE

Inside-forward Ernie Machin joined the Sky Blues from Nelson in March 1962 and a year later made his league debut for the club in a 2–0 home win over Millwall. After a good start to the 1963–64 season Machin was hampered by a series of knee injuries which restricted his number of appearances as he pushed for international recognition. In fact his injured knee kept him out for over half the following season, and it was 1965–66 before he won a regular place in the City side.

Ernie Machin.

When Coventry won the Second Division Championship in 1966–67 Machin was the club's second highest scorer with eleven goals. He was one of City's most consistent performers in the top flight and although he was still troubled by his knee, he had scored thirty nine goals in 289 games when he joined Plymouth Argyle in December 1972 for £35,000. He later played for Brighton and Hove Albion before returning to Highfield Road for a short spell as the club's youth team coach.

MACKAY, DON

During his playing days Don Mackay was a goalkeeper, beginning his career with Forfar Athletic. He was transferred to Dundee United in 1969 and made forty nine league appearances before trying his luck in England with Southend United.

After hanging up his gloves he turned his attention to coaching and worked with Bristol City before accepting ther manager's job at Dens Park, the home of Dundee. After taking the side to promotion to the Premier League and to a League Cup Final, he moved to Coventry City as assistant to Bobby Gould. When Gould left Highfield Road, Mackay took over with Frank Upton as his assistant. The two seasons were spent successfully staving off relegation but towards the end of the 1985–86 season he resigned after the club had gone eight games without a win.

He returned to Scotland to run the reserve and youth side for Graeme Souness at Rangers. Then in February 1987 he was installed as Blackburn Rover's manager with the Ewood Park club anchored to the foot of the Second Division table. He steered Rovers to a Full Members' Cup victory at Wembley and displayed boldness and courage in persuading players of the calibre of Ardilles and Archibald to join the club. Mackay took the Lancashire club to the brink of the top flight on three successive occasions but he was the victim of his own success and was sacked in 1991. He later managed Fulham for three years.

MANAGERS

Here is the complete list of City's full-time managers with the inclusive dates in which they held office:

Harry Pollitt	1920–1921	Noel Cantwell	1968–1972
Albert Evans	1921–1925	Bob Dennison	1972
James Kerr	1926–1928	Joe Mercer	1972–1974
James McIntyre	1928–1931	Gordon Milne	1974–1981
Harry Storer	1931–1945	Dave Sexton	1981–1983
Dick Bayliss	1946–1947	Bobby Gould	1983–1984
Billy Frith	1947–1949	Don Mackay	1984–1986
Jack Fairbrother	1954–1955	George Curtis	1986–1987
Charlie Elliott	1954–1955	John Sillett	1987–1990
Jesse Carver	1955–1956	Terry Butcher	1990–1992
George Raynor	1955–1956	Don Howe	1992
Harry Warren	1957–1958	Bobby Gould	1992–1993
Billy Frith	1958–1962	Phil Neal	1993–1995
Jimmy Hill	1962–1968	Ron Atkinson	1995–1996
		Gordon Strachan	1996–

MARATHON MATCHES

Coventry City have been involved in four FA Cup games that have gone to three matches. These were Carlisle United (Preliminary Round 1908–09), Reading (Second Round 1932–33), Portsmouth (Fourth Round 1962–63) and Wolverhampton Wanderers (Third Round 1983–84).

MARKSMEN – LEAGUE

Coventry City's top league goal scorer is Clarrie Bourton who struck 171 league goals during his seven seasons at Highfield Road. Only he and Billy Lake have scored more than 100 league goals for the club.

1	Clarrie Bourton	171
2	Billy Lake	113
3	Ted Roberts	85
4	Frank Herbert	84
5	Ray Straw	79
6	Peter Hill	73
7	Leslie Jones	70
8	George Hudson	62
9	Jock Lauderdal	60
10	Ian Wallace	58

MARKSMEN – OVERALL

The club's top marksman is Clarrie Bourton who scored 180 goals in all competitions for the club.

1	Clarrie Bourton	180
2	Billy Lake	123
3	Frank Herbert	88
4	Ted Roberts	87
5	Ray Straw	85
6	Peter Hill	77
7	George Hudson	75
8	Leslie Jones	74
9	Jock Lauderdale	63
10	Cyrille Regis	62

MARTIN, NEIL

Neil Martin served an apprenticeship as a mining engineer at Alloa before later playing for Queen of the South and Hibernians. He was very good in the air and became a prolific goal scorer at Easter Road, netting forty goals in 1964–65. He had scored seventy eight goals in Scottish football when, in October 1965, Sunderland manager Ian McColl paid Hibernian

£50,000 for his services. He scored on his debut in a 3–1 win over Sheffield Wednesday but it was the following season when he hit his best form, top–-scoring with twenty six goals in forty eight League and Cup games. His total included hat-tricks against Blackpool (Home 4–0) and Peterborough United (Home 7–1). He went on to score forty six goals in 100 games for the Wearsiders before joining Coventry City in February 1968.

He made his debut for the Sky Blues in a 2–1 home win over Chelsea, going on to score eight goals in fifteen games, including a hat-trick in a 3–0 win over Sheffield Wednesday. Having helped to save the club from relegation, he proceeded to do the same in 1968–69, his most important strike being a last minute winner at Leicester City. In 1969–70 he was the club's top scorer with fourteen league goals as City finished sixth in the First Division.

He went on to score forty five goals in122 games at Highfield Road before surprisingly being allowed to join Nottingham Forest. He was hampered by injuries at the City Ground and moved on to have spells with both Brighton and Crystal Palace.

He was joint manager with Ian Buckley at Walsall for a while, having previously been the youth team coach, but in his only season in charge the Saddlers just avoided relegation by one place on goal difference.

MASON, GEORGE

Centre-half George Mason joined Coventry from Redhill Amateurs and though he made his first team debut in a 3–1 defeat at Bristol Rovers in March 1932, he had to wait until midway through the 1934–35 season before winning a regular place. City manager Harry Storer made Mason the club's captain and in 1935–36 he led Coventry to the Third Division (South) Championship. Over the next three seasons, the club pushed hard for promotion to the top flight and Mason missed just four games in 1937–38, being ever-present in the other two seasons.

The giant centre–half lost his best years to the Second World War but in 1942 he represented England in two unofficial wartime internationals. When league football resumed in 1946–47, Mason was still the club's first–choice pivot and went on to play in 350 League and Cup games, making his last appearance against West Ham United in February 1952, some twenty one years after joining the club.

MASON, DICK

After playing his early football with Arley Miners' Welfare, Dick Mason joined Nuneaton Borough, from where Coventry signed him in the summer of 1946. He made his debut at left-half in a 3–1 defeat at Newcastle United on 11 September 1946 and went on to appear in twenty four league games in that campaign. Towards the end of that season he was converted to left-back and was a virtual ever-present in that position for the next six seasons.

Strong in the tackle and a good distributor of the ball, Mason scored two goals for City during his time at Highfield Road but in neither game did the club come out on top. He had appeared in 263 League and Cup games when, in the early part of the 1953–54 season, he lost his place in the City defence to Roy Kirk and after a season in the club's reserve side, he moved to Bedworth Town as player/manager.

MATCH OF THE DAY

Coventry City's first appearance on BBC's *Match of the Day* was on 7 May 1966 when they won 2–0 at Huddersfield Town in a Second Division match with Bobby Gould and Ray Pointer scoring the Sky Blues' goals.

MATTHEWS, REG

Coventry's first international, Reg Matthews, had been signed by Billy Frith from the ground staff team, Modern Machine Tools, on his seventeenth birthday in 1950, but had to wait three years before making his league debut in a 1–0 defeat at Southend United. Even then he only played in a handful of games and it was not until 1954–55 that he had a lengthy run in the team following an injury to Peter Taylor.

He was one of the early 'keepers to start an attack by throwing the ball out to a colleague and soon became the undisputed star of an ailing Coventry side. He progressed through the England ranks at Under-23 and

'B' level but with England having an embarrassing supply of international class goalkeepers such as Gil Merrick, Bert Williams and Ron Baynham, there were many who thought that it would be impossible for a Third Division player to break into the England side.

However, with some outstanding performances for Coventry keeping him in the headlines, he eventually made his full international debut against Scotland at Hampden Park in April 1956 and gave a creditable performance in a 1–1 draw. Matthews made another four international appearances against Brazil, Sweden, Germany and Northern Ireland before it became quite evident that City would have to cash in on their talent despite the club's directors denying the possibility.

In November 1956, after he had made 116 League and Cup appearances, he left the club for Chelsea for a then record fee for a goalkeeper of £22,500. After five years at Stamford Bridge in which he made 135 League appearances, he moved to Derby County and made 247 appearances for the Rams before leaving the Baseball Ground in 1968 to become player/manager of Rugby Town.

MERCER, JOE

One of the game's all-time greats, Joe Mercer had a great career both as a player and a manager. He began his career as a junior with Everton in 1932 and stayed with them until 1946. In that time he developed into one of the finest wing-halves in the country and helped the Merseyside club to the League Championship in 1938–39. He lost seven seasons of top class soccer but played regularly in wartime soccer, being part of a famous England half-back line with Cullis and Britton. Out of favour with Everton, he moved to Arsenal where his career was rejuvenated. He led the Gunners to the League Championship in 1947–48 and played in his first FA Cup Final for the club in 1950 when they beat Liverpool. Mercer was voted Footballer of the Year in 1950 and won another League Championship medal in 1952–53. His illustrious career came to an end when he broke his leg in April 1954 while playing against Blackpool just before his fortieth birthday.

Mercer went into management, first with Sheffield United and then Aston Villa. At Villa Park he saw the club promoted from the Second

Division, reach two FA Cup semi-finals and win the League Cup. However, in 1964, Mercer suffered a stroke due to overwork. The Villa directors waited until he was over the worst effects, then sacked him.

In July 1965 he made a comeback as manager of Manchester City. Along with Malcolm Allison he revitalised the club. They won the Second Division title in 1965–66, then the League Championship two years later. More trophies followed in the shape of the FA Cup in 1969 and the European Cup Winners' Cup in 1970.

In June 1972 Mercer moved to become general manager of Coventry City with Gordon Milne as team manager. In 1974 he took temporary charge of the England team. He was awarded an OBE for his services to football in 1976, a year after he had been made a director of Coventry City. He resigned from the Coventry board after six years and lived in retirement on Merseyside until his death in August 1990.

MILNE, GORDON

Gordon Milne began his playing career with non-league Morecambe before following in his father's footsteps by playing for Preston North End. In September 1960 he was transferred to Liverpool for £17,000. He made a strong contribution to Liverpool's successful Second Division Championship-winning season of 1961–62 by playing in all forty two matches. He went on to play in 279 games for Liverpool, also gaining two League Championship medals and playing in the European Cup Winners' Cup Final against Borussia Dortmund in May 1966. On leaving Anfield he joined Blackpool where he ended his league career.

He enjoyed a long career in management starting with Wigan Athletic which he led to the Northern Premier League title in 1970–71. After a spell as the manager of the England Youth team, during which it won the 1972 European Youth tournament, he joined Coventry City as team manager under Joe Mercer.

At Highfield Road, Milne produced some fine players through the club's youth scheme but his sides never really fulfilled their potential and the Coventry board and fans lost patience with him. In August 1982 he was released by the club after spending his last fifteen months as executive manager dealing with contracts and transfers.

He joined Leicester City and in 1982–83 took the Foxes into the First Division. Eventually sacked at Filbert Street, he moved to Turkey where he enjoyed great success with Besiktas.

MORGAN, BILL

Goalkeeper Bill Morgan played his early football for his local club in the north-east, Mickley Colliery, and had just had an outstanding game against Blyth Spartans in an FA Cup qualifying round in 1931–32 when Coventry manager, Harry Storer, persuaded him to join the Highfield Road club.

He made his debut in a 2–2 draw at Cardiff City towards the end of the following season, keeping his place for the last eight games of the campaign. After making just twenty six appearances in his first four seasons with the club, he was ever-present in 1936–37 when it finished eighth in Division Two. He missed just one game in each of the next two campaigns, with the club finishing fourth in Division Two on both occasions. Over those three seasons, Morgan kept forty six clean sheets in League and Cup matches and so not surprisingly Coventry City received a number of offers for his services from top flight clubs, but with the coming of the Second World War nothing developed.

He had appeared in 156 games when war broke out but continued to keep goal for the club in regional league games, playing in fifty two matches until dislocating his shoulder at Leicester in October 1943. After retiring in January 1944 he stayed at the club as trainer before joining Modern Machines FC in a similar capacity.

MORGAN, J G

Often referred to as 'the Father of the Club' J G Morgan became its secretary in 1887, the first non-player to take over this role. He was a director of the Singer Cycle Works and had a tobacconist shop on the opposite side of Canterbury Street. Once a week a large crowd would gather at Morgan's tobacconist shop to see his team selection for the match the following Saturday.

During his six years with the club, Morgan transformed each and every aspect associated with it. The club became one of the most respected junior sides in the Midlands, playing in front of crowds numbering several thousand. When Morgan retired in 1893, Singers had won almost everything there was to win at their level.

MORTIMER, DENNIS

Dennis Mortimer joined Coventry City's apprentice staff in the summer of 1967 and after working his way up through the ranks, made his league debut as a substitute in a 2–2 draw at home to West Ham United in October 1969. Later that season he captained the Sky Blues Youth team to the FA Youth Cup Final where they lost  to Tottenham Hotspur over four matches. When he was with Coventry he played six times for the England Under-23 side and in the match against Holland scored twice in a 3–1 win. He had scored twelve goals in 222 League and Cup games for City when he left Highfield Road in December 1975 and joined Aston Villa for £175,000.

With the Villans, Mortimer won a League Cup winners' tankard in 1977 and winners' medals in the club's successes in the First Division, European Cup and European Super Cup competitions in 1981 and 1982. In 1980 he captained the England 'B' side in

Dennis Mortimer.

Australia and was desperately unlucky not to win full international honours. An ever-present for Villa in seasons 1977–78 and 1980–81, he appeared in 404 matches, scoring thirty six goals, before joining Brighton and Hove Albion at the end of the 1984–85 season. He later had a season with Birmingham City but then retired from league football.

MOST MATCHES

Coventry City played their greatest number of matches, fifty seven, in the season 1962–63. There were forty six league games, nine FA Cup games and two League Cup games.

MURPHY, PETER

Inside-forward Peter Murphy was on Birmingham's books as an amateur before signing professional forms for Coventry City. He made his debut for the Highfield Road club in a 1–0 home win over Fulham in December 1946 but it was midway through the following season before he won a regular place in the Coventry side. He formed a prolific goal scoring partnership with Ted Roberts and scored thirteen goals in thrity six games in 1948–49 before topping the club's scoring charts the following season. His total of fifteen goals included hat-tricks in the wins over Chesterfield (Home 3–0) and West Ham United (Home 5–1). He had scored thirty seven goals in 119 games when he was rather surprisingly sold to Spurs for £18,500. After helping the White Hart Lane club to win the League Championship, he lost his place in the side and joined Birmingham City for £20,000.

He scored a hat-trick on his debut for the St Andrew's club as Doncaster Rovers were beaten 5–0. In 1952–53 he set a new post-war goal scoring record for the club w ith twenty six goals in thirty eight games including hat-tricks against Leicester City (Away 4–3) and Oldham Athletic (Away 3–1). When the Blues won the Second Division Championship in 1954–55 Murphy was top scorer with twenty goals. The following season he helped the club reach the FA Cup Final, scoring in each of the four rounds up to the semi-final. In 1957–58, Murphy was once again Birmingham's leading scorer with twenty three goals, including another hat-trick in a 4–0 home win over Manchester City. After scoring 127 goals in 278 games he returned to Highfield Road where he had a spell on the club's coaching staff before going into the licensing trade and working as a representative for Davenport's brewery.

N

NDLOVU, PETER

A Zimbabwe international from the age of fifteen, Peter Ndlovu was spotted by Coventry City during their summer tour of that country in 1990. After being invited for a trial, he signed a contract the following summer. He made his league debut for the Sky Blues in a 1–1 draw at Queen's Park Rangers in August 1991. After topping the club's scoring charts with eleven goals in 1993–94, Ndlovu formed a prolific goal scoring partnership with Dion Dublin the following season, again netting eleven goals. His total in 1994–95 included his first hat-trick for the club in a 3–2 win at Liverpool.

Despite all the travelling he had to do when called upon to represent Zimbabwe in African Nation Cup matches, Ndlovu scored some brilliant goals for the Sky Blues. The highly talented striker or midfield player has amazing ball control and devastating pace. Sadly his progress at Highfield Road was hampered by a knee injury picked up when on international duty for Zimbabwe in the summer of 1996. Two operations followed before he regained his place in the side but in July 1997, after scoring forty one goals in 196 games, he was allowed to join Birmingham City.

Signed on a pay-as-you-play deal, the Zimbabwean international scored four times in his first six games for the St Andrew's club before suffering a loss of form. He later returned to something like his best, ending his first season with eleven goals in forty six games.

NEAL, PHIL

Beginning his career with Northampton Town, Phil Neal made 206 appearances for the Cobblers before joining Liverpool for £65,000 in October 1974. He made his debut against Everton the following month and, from his second appearance in December 1974, he played in 366 consecutive league games. An intelligent positional player, Neal's distribution was immaculate. The most capped England right-back, with fifty to his name, he won almost every honour while playing for Liverpool including seven League Championship medals. He was on the winning side in four League Cup finals and had a UEFA Cup winners' medal and four European Cup winners' Cup medals – only an FA Cup winners' medal eluded him.

In December 1985 he left Anfield to join Bolton Wanderers as player/manager. His first few years in management were quite eventful. In 1986 he led the side to Wembley in the Freight Rover Trophy Final and although they were relegated to the Fourth Division in 1986–87 they bounced back at the end of the following campaign. He took the Wanderers to Wembley again in 1989 when they beat Torquay United 4–1 to win the Sherpa Van Trophy. On leaving Burnden Park, Neal had a period of involvement with the England management team before taking charge of Coventry City in November 1993.

His appointment helped to steady the team and they finished the 1993–94 season in eleventh place. Midway through the following campaign City failed to beat a number of fellow strugglers and in February 1995 this led to the departure of Neal by mutual consent. A year later he took charge of Cardiff City before becoming caretaker/manager of Manchester City.

NEUTRAL GROUNDS

Highfield Road has been used as a neutral ground for FA Cup matches on a number of occasions. Coventry themselves have only had to replay on a neutral ground twice:

Date	Opponents	Venue	Score
19.12.1932	Reading	Stamford Bridge	0–1
19.03.1963	Portsmouth	White Hart Lane	2–1

The club's FA Cup semi-final match against Leeds United in 1987 was played at Hillsborough and its appearance in that season's final at Wembley also qualifies for inclusion.

NICKNAMES

Coventry City's nickname is the Sky Blues. Many players in the club's history have been fondly known by their nicknames, including:

Ernie Boston	1908–1914	Konk
Fred Turnbull	1911–1912	Boxer
Ernie Toseland	1928–1929	Twinkletoes
Frank Herbert	1922–1929	Cute
George Curtis	1955–1969	The Ironman
Ray Straw	1957–1961	Toffee
Chris Cattlin	1968–1976	Spider
Brian Borrows	1985–1997	Bugsy

NO GOAL!

When Coventry played Bury on 11 October 1947 George Lowrie, the City centreforward who possessed a powerful shot, hit the back of the Shakers' net – and the ball burst. The referee refused to allow the goal and the game, watched by a crowd of 25,577, finished goal-less.

NON-LEAGUE

Coventry have played non-league clubs in the FA Cup on a number of occasions. The most recent was the third round replay match against Woking on 4 February 1997 which City won 2–1. The club's record against non-league opposition since it joined the Football League is.

Date	Opposition	Venue	Stage	Score
28.11.1925	Worksop	Away	Round 1	0–1
27.11.1926	Kettering Town	Away	Round 1	3–2
14.12.1929	Bath City	Home	Round 2	7–1
26.11.1932	Guildford	Away	Round 1	2–1
06.12.1952	Bishop Auckland	Away	Round 2	4–1
16.11.1957	Walthamstow Avenue	Home	Round 1	1–0
16.11.1958	Weymouth	Away	Round 1	5–2
05.11.1960	Worcester City	Away	Round 1	4–1
25.11.1961	King's Lynn	Home	Round 2	1–2
16.11.1963	Trowbridge	Away	Round 1	6–1
08.01.1982	Worcester City	Home	Round 3	3–1
07.01.1988	Sutton United	Away	Round 3	1–2
25.01.1997	Woking	Home	Round 3	1–1
04.0.1997	Woking	Away	Round 3(R)	2–1

O

OGRIZOVIC, STEVE

The son of an immigrant Yugoslav miner, goalkeeper Steve Ogrizovic began his Football League career with Chesterfield and made his debut for the Spireites against Port Vale in August 1977. After keeping six clean sheets in the opening sixteen games of the 1977–78 season, his potential was spotted by Liverpool who paid £70,000 for his services in November 1977.

Steve Ogrizovic

His role at Anfield was as understudy to Ray Clemence and after only four games in five years he was involved in a straight swap for Bob Wardle, the Shrewsbury goalkeeper. He spent two seasons, both as everpresents, at Gay Meadow before Coventry paid £72,000 to bring him to Highfield Road in the summer of 1984. After making his Sky Blues debut in a 1–0 defeat at Aston Villa on the opening day of the 1984–85 season, he played in 209 consecutive league games to equal Alf Wood's club record.

On 25 October 1986 he became the first Coventry goalkeeper to score a league goal when his long kick upfield bounced over Martin Hodge in the Sheffield Wednesday goal to earn the Sky Blues a point in a 2–2 draw. That season saw him win an FA Cup winners' medal when Coventry beat Spurs 3–2 in the Wembley final.

Since then Steve Ogrizovic has been a model of consistency, missing very few games despite breaking a leg in 1995. He went on to beat George Curtis' all-time appearance record, playing in 598 first team games. In 1998 was awarded the PFA Merit award for achievements to the game, before in the spring of 2000 making two more appearances at the age of 42.

OLDEST PLAYER

The oldest player to line up in a Coventry City team is Alf Wood. He was 44 years 207 days old when he played his last game for the club against Plymouth Argyle in a second round FA Cup match on 7 December 1958. The Aldridge-born 'keeper who had played his first game for the club some twenty years earlier, was on the losing side as City went down 3–1 in front of a Highfield Road crowd of 27,295.

OVERSEAS PLAYERS

Coventry City have had a number of overseas players on their books. Probably the first from overseas to play for the club was Emilio Aldecoa, a Spanish international who played twenty nine games in 1946–47.

Belgian international, winger Roger Van Gool, joined Coventry from FC Cologne in March 1980 but failed to score in any of his nineteen first team games. Rudi Kaiser came to Highfield Road from Antwerp in the summer of 1981 and scored three goals in sixteen league games in the 1981–82 season. Yugoslavian international, Raddy Avramovic, joined the Sky Blues from Inter Montreal and played in eighteen games during the 1983–84 season. Jose Perdom, who was a Uruguayan international, joined Coventry on a non-contract basis from Italian club Genoa but only made four league appearances.

Zimbabwean international, Peter Ndlovu, joined Coventry from the Highlanders for £10,000 in the summer of 1991. The highly talented player netted forty one goals in 197 games for City before leaving to play for Birmingham. German midfielder Detzi Kruszynski, who also played for Wimbledon and Brentford, appeared in two games for the club in 1993–94. The next overseas player to join the Sky Blues was Marques Isaias, a Brazilian-born midfielder who was signed from Benfica in the 1995 close season for £500,000. Sadly, most of his time at Highfield Road was spent on the treatment table.

Ukraine international central defender, Alex Evtushok, arrived at Highfield Road for a fee of £800,000 from Karpaty but failed to settle and left after playing in three games. Belgain international full-back Regis Genaux was signed from Standard Liege in the summer of 1996 but only made four Premier League appearances before being sold to

Udinese. Dutch Under-21 captain, George Boateng, signed for Coventry from Feyenoord and made an immediate impact continuing his outstanding performances throughout the 1998–99 season.

Swedish international goalkeeper, Marcus Hedman, finally replaced Steve Ogrizovic in December 1997 and has been a virtual ever-present since then. The brother of Bolton's Michael, Martin Johansen a Danish international, has just made a handful of appearances for the club.

Viorel Moldavan became the club's record buy when he joined them from Grasshoppers of Zurich for £3.25 million. The Romanian international had a good World Cup, scoring in the 2–1 win over England. However, he was soon on his way out of Highfield Road joining Fenerbahce for £4 million. Capped ninety four times by Sweden, Roland Nilsson returned to English football when he joined the Sky Blues from Helsingborg and added much needed experience to the Coventry back four. Norwegian international, Trond Soltvedt, made a good impression on the English game following his arrival from Rosenborg Trondheim.

In 1998–99 City had a number of new overseas players on their books. Philippe Clement from Gent arrived at Highfield Road and Jean Guy Wallemme signed from Lens but after making six appearances left to join Sochaux. Goalkeeper Morton Hyldgaard joined the club from Ikast for £250,000, thus strengthening the Sky Blues' reargurard. Belgian teenage ace, Laurent Delorge, joined Coventry from Gent for a fee of £1.25 million and City paid £2 million for the services of Mohammed Konjic from Monaco.

In the summer of 1999, Gordon Strachan signed two Moroccan internationals – Youssef Chippo and Mustapha Hadji, the latter from Deportivo La Coruna for a club record £4 million.

Other players with foreign-sounding surnames include Steve Pgrizovic, Peter Bodak, Peter Hormantschuk, Frank Kletzenbauer and Robert Rosario – they were all born in the British Isles.

OWN GOALS

When Coventry played hosts to Leyton Orient on 20 September 1954, centre-half Roy Kirk put through his own goal twice in the 2–2 draw.

Jeff Blockley's last match for the Sky Blues on 30 September 1972 saw him score a spectacular own goal in a 3–1 defeat against Chelsea when he chipped Bill Glazier from fully 30 yards. However, these performances pale into insignificance when compared to Jackie Randle's misdemeanours. He holds the most unenviable record concerning own goals, for on 18 September 1926 he netted all three goals for Bristol City in a 3–0 win over Coventry at Ashton Gate.

P

PARKES, HARRY

Harry Parkes played his football for Halesowen before signing for West Bromwich Albion in the summer of 1906. When only seventeen he played in the club's semi-final against Everton but in December 1908, after a dispute over terms, he joined Coventry City. He made his debut for the club in a 1–1 draw against Swindon Town on Christmas Day but over the next two seasons only appeared in twenty two Southern League games due to the consistency of the club's regular outside-right, Charlie Tickle.

He won a regular place in the City side at the start of the 1910–11 season and ended the campaign as the club's top scorer with eleven goals. He headed the club's scoring charts for a second time in 1912–13 when his total of twelve goals in thirty eight league games included a hat-trick in a 4–1 home win over West Ham United.

He had scored thirty eight goals in 170 games when he left Highfield Road, following the club's dreadful season of 1913–14 when it finished bottom of the Southern League First Division, to return to West Bromwich Albion. During the war he acted as player/assistant manager of the Baggies but in 1919 he became secretary/manager of Newport County. After three seasons with the Welsh club he joined Chesterfield as manager before taking over the reins at Lincoln City. He led the Imps to the Third Division (North) Championship in 1931–32 but following their relegation he left to manage Mansfield Town. Failing to find success at Field Mill, he joined Notts County where he ended his involvement with the game in 1939.

PEAKE, TREVOR

Trevor Peake played his early football for non-league Nuneaton Borough where he won international recognition by playing for England at semi-professional level. He was twenty two when he joined Lincoln City, going on to play in 171 league games for the Sincil Bank club before signing for Coventry City in the summer of 1983.

His first game for the Sky Blues was in a 1–1 draw at Spurs in the second match of the 1983–84 season. Peake went on to serve Coventry for the next eight seasons, missing very few matches. In 1984–85, when he was the club's captain, he formed a formidable central defensive partnership with Brian Kilcline. However, he was stripped of the captaincy after two seasons at Highfield Road following a disagreement with manager, Don Mackay.

Trevor Peake.

Peake won an FA Cup winners' medal in 1987 when he was the club's most outstanding player in the 3–2 win over Spurs and the following season almost won international recognition when he was selected for the England 'B' team, but had to withdraw due to injury. He went on to appear in 331 games for Coventry before being allowed to join Luton Town in the summer of 1991. He went on to play in 202 games for the Hatters where he later became reserve team coach. In September 1997, at the age of forty, he became the club's oldest league player. Peake is now back at Highfield Road as the club's coach.

PITCH

The Highfield Road pitch measures 110 yards by 75 yards.

PLASTIC

There have been four Football League clubs that replaced their normal grass playing pitches with artificial surfaces at one stage or another. Queen's Park Rangers were the first in 1981 but the Loftus Road plastic was discarded in 1988 in favour of a return to turf. Luton Town, Oldham

Athletic and Preston North End followed. Coventry never played on the Boundary Park or Deepdale plastic but met Queen's Park Rangers on the Loftus Road plastic on five occasions, winning twice. In 1985–86, City won 2–0 at Loftus Road and 1–0 on Luton's Kenilworth Road plastic. The club also played five times at Luton, winning two and drawing one of the meetings.

POINTS

Under the three points for a win system which was introduced in 1981–82 Coventry City's best points tally is sixty three in 1986–87 when they finished tenth in Division One. However, the club's best points haul under the old two points for a win system is sixty in the seasons of 1958–59 and 1963–64 when the Sky Blues finished runners-up in the Fourth Division and Third Division Champions respectively. Those performances would have netted the club eighty four points in 1958–59 and eighty two in 1963–64.

Coventry's worst record under either system was the meagre twenty nine points secured in 1919–20, the club's first season in the Football League.

POLLITT, HARRY

Very little is known about Harry Pollitt before and after he joined Coventry City as manager. When he came to the club it was firmly rooted at the foot of the Second Division and had not won a match. Pollitt was given the then unbelievable sum of £5,000 to spend on new players.

Despite managing to steer Coventry clear of relegation, the club finishing in twentiethth place, Pollitt still lost his job. It later transpired that he had helped to set up a 'fix' in the final game of the season against Bury when Coventry needed to win to avoid having to apply for re–election. His implication in the 'Bury Scandal' was not unearthed for a further five years at which time he was banned *sine die*.

POSTPONED

The bleak winter of 1962–63, described at the time as the 'Modern Ice

Age', proved to be one of the most chaotic seasons in British soccer. The worst Saturday for league action in that awful winter was 9 February when only seven Football League fixtures went ahead. The worst Saturday for the FA Cup was 5 January, the day of the third round, when only three of the thirty two ties could be played. Lincoln City v Coventry City had to be postponed fifteen times and was eventually played on 7 March 1963 with the Sky Blues winning 5–1 at Sincil Bank.

POWELL, BARRY

The son of a Welsh international wing-half ,Ivor Powell, midfielder Barry Powell began his Football League career with Wolves. He established himself as a regular during 1973–74 and picked up a winners' medal in Wolves' victory over Manchester City in the League Cup Final of 1974. A few days later he won the first of five England Under-23 caps as they beat Scotland 2–0. After spending the summer of 1975 in America with Portland Timbers, he joined Coventry City for £75,000 in September 1975. He made his debut in a 3–1 League Cup victory over Bolton Wanderers and went on to play in most of the club's games over the next five seasons, being ever-present in 1977–78. The club's regular penalty taker, he scored twenty nine goals in 180 League and Cup games for the Sky Blues before being transferred to Derby County for £340,000 in October 1979.

The Rams were relegated at the end of Powell's first season at the Baseball Ground and he left to play in Hong Kong for Bulova. Two years later he returned to England to play for Burnley. After a spell at Swansea he returned to his first club, Wolves, where he ended his playing career before being appointed to the Molineux coaching staff.

He is now back at Highfield Road as the club's Football in the Community Officer.

PREMIER LEAGUE

Coventry City made a sensational start to the first season of Premier League football in 1992–93 when, after seven games, they lay in fifth position. By mid-October the Sky Blues had moved up to third but began to slip down the table after the turn of the year. They remained in the top ten until the closing stages of the season when the team slipped and ended the campaign in fifteenth place after a series of bad results.

As in the previous season, 1993–94 began in brilliant fashion with a 3–0 win at Arsenal on the opening day. The Sky Blues took the Premier League's longest unbeaten run from the start of the season, going until their ninth game before they lost 2–0 at Leeds United. In October, manager Bobby Gould quit following rumours that the board were going to sell Zimbabwean Peter Ndlovu. Phil Neal was appointed manager and he helped steady the team, but after injury to Roy Wegerle results were mixed. After beating Cup finalists Chelsea 2–1 and holding double winners ,Manchester United, to a goal-less draw at Old Trafford, City finished in eleventh place.

After a disappointing start to the 1994–95 season the Sky Blues put together a run of five wins and two draws that took them into the top half of the table. However, that was followed by eleven matches without a win and resulted in the departure, by mutual consent, of Phil Neal. Ron Atkinson took over and although the side failed to sustain their form of March when the new City boss won the Manager of the Month award, they ended the season in sixteenth place, safe from relegation.

In 1995–96, the Sky Blues recorded just one win in the opening sixteen fixtures and were firmly at the foot of the table. They climbed out of the relegation zone just after Christmas but then found themselves second from bottom with just a handful of games remaining. In fact the Sky Blues left Premiership survival until the last day of the season when their safety was guaranteed courtesy of a goal-less home draw against Leeds United.

The following season saw City take just one point from their opening five matches before beating Leeds United 2–1. After a 1–0 defeat at Sunderland the club embarked on a run of six successive draws followed by three defeats. These results saw them firmly entrenched in the bottom three. In November Atkinson moved upstairs and Gordon Strachan his assistant took over as manager. The club's fortunes did not change and only one win in twelve games made Coventry favouites for the drop. However, results improved and once again they needed favourable results on the final day of the season. The Sky Blues beat Spurs 2–1 and thanks to Sunderland losing to a late Wimbledon goal, survived by one point.

The 1997–98 season saw Coventry reach their joint highest Premiership position of eleventh and their second highest Premiership points total. The club made a great start to the season, winning 3–2 at home to Chelsea with Dion Dublin netting a hat-trick. However, by the end of October Coventry was the only club in the entire Football League still to score on its travels. Coventry then put that record straight with a 2–1 win at Wimbledon. After losing at Chelsea early in the New Year, they were not to lose another league match until April – a run of nine matches which included a 5–1 win at Bolton. The club drew a great many of its last games, ending the campaign with just one defeat in their last fifteen matches.

The 1998–99 season was a disappointment for the Sky Blues. They were again forced to struggle against relegation, and if Whelan and Huckerby had not been amongst the goals, they would surely have ended their long stay in the top flight. As it was City, who were undefeated in the last three games of the season, finished fifteenth on forty two points.

PROMOTION

Coventry City have been promoted on four occasions. The first was in 1935–36 when they won the Third Division (South) Championship. City were beaten just once at Highfield Road when Aldershot won 2–0 on Christmas Day. They scored 102 goals with their biggest wins being 8–1 over Crystal Palace, 7–1 over Newport County and 6–1 over Queen's Park Rangers, but only secured promotion with a 2–1 defeat of Torquay United.

The club gaind promotion a second time in 1958–59 when it finished the season as runners-up to Port Vale in the Fourth Division with a then record points total of sixty. Again it only lost one home game, going down 2–1 to Carlisle United. However, it made amends in the return at Brunton Park, winning 6–1.

In 1963–64, Coventry won the Third Division Championship, equalling their record points total and clinching the title with a 1–0 home win over Colchester United on the final day of the season.

The club's final experience of promotion was in 1966–67 when the Sky Blues won the Second Division Championship. Again the club lost just one game at Highfield Road with Crystal Palace winning 2–1.

111

Q

QUINN, MICK

An old-fashioned striker who entered League football with Wigan Athletic, scoring on his debut in a 3–1 win over Halifax Town in April 1980. Although he helped the Latics to win promotion to the Third

Division, he was released and joined Stockport County. He was an immediate success at Edgeley Park, becoming the first County player for fifteen years to top twenty goals in a season.

He maintained his prolific scoring rate in 1983–84 but at the end of the season, after having scored forty one goals in seventy games, he was snapped up by Oldham Athletic. As with his former clubs, Quinn was the leading goal scorer, but in March 1986 the then struggling Lancashire club sold him to Portsmouth for £150,000.

After just missing out on promotion in 1986–87

'Old fashioned striker' Mike Quinn in action Pompey made no mistake the following season, with Quinn scoring twenty two goals in the League and six in the Cup competitions. After Portsmouth lasted just one season in the top flight and then fell straight back into the Third Division Quinn, who had scored sixty eight goals in 139 games for the Fratton Park club, opted to leave them at the end of his contract.

He joined Newcastle United, the fee of £680,000 being decided by the Transfer Tribunal. He made a sensational start for the Magpies, scoring four times on his debut against Leeds United and ending the campaign with thirty two league goals. He had scored seventy one goals in 140 games for the St James Park club when following a spell on loan with Coventry City, he joined the Highfield Road club on a permanent basis.

If anything Quinn's start at Highfield Road was even more sensational than his Newcastle debut. After scoring twice on his debut, he proceeded to amass ten goals in his first six starts including two in a 5–1 demolition of Liverpool. Despite a barren spell midway through the campaign, he ended the season with seventeen goals in twenty six games. In 1993–94, Quinn netted a hat-trick on the opening day of the season as they beat Arsenal 3–0 at Highbury. There followed loan spells at Plymouth and Portsmouth before Quinn, who had scored twenty six goals in sixty eight games for the Sky Blues, left Highfield Road.

R

RAPID SCORING

On 4 March 1933 Coventry City led Queen's Park Rangers 7–0 at half time in a Third Division (South) game with goals from Lake (3) Bourton (2) Lauderdale and Richards. There was no further scoring in the second half.

RAYNOR, GEORGE

George Raynor was a speedy, clever winger who played his football for Mansfield Town, Rotherham United, Bury and Aldershot. During the Second World War he served in the Middle East and organised football in Baghdad. Unable to find a coaching job in England, he was recommended to the Swedish FA by Sir Stanley Rous. On taking over the running of the national squad, he led them to success in the Olympic Games of 1948 and in 1950 took them to the World Cup semi-finals. He left Sweden in 1954 to go into Italian football where he coached both Roma and Lazio. He was at Lazio when Coventry manager, Jesse Carver, persuaded him to move to Highfield Road. Raynor was put in charge of team training and match preparation and when Carver left the club to return to Italy, he was the ideal replacement. However, Raynor met with plenty of interference from the club's directors and he resigned soon after being demoted to chief coach to accommodate general manager, Harry Warren.

Raynor rejoined the Swedish FA and coached the national side to the 1958 World Cup Final where they lost 5–2 to Brazil. He later managed Doncaster Rovers who went on to win the Fourth Division Championship shortly after his departure.

RECEIPTS

The club's record receipts are £375,510 for the FA Cup sixth round match against Sheffield United at Highfield Road on 7 March 1998. Coventry

City still have a memento of their mid-week match at Merthyr Tydfil's Penydarren Park in April 1930, the Welsh club's last season in the Football League. It is a cheque for their share of the receipts, amounting to 18s 4d (92p). For the record, the attendance was 683.

REES, RONNIE

Ronnie Rees began his Football League career with Coventry City and made his debut for the Sky Blues in a goal-less home draw against

Shrewsbury Town in September 1962. After that he became a fixture in the Highfield Road club's first team for the next six seasons. Able to play on either wing, Rees won international recognition in 1962 when he won Welsh Under-23 honours before winning the first of thirty nine caps for his country when he played against Scotland in 1965. His best season for the club in terms of goals scored was 1963–64 when he was ever-present as Coventry won the Third Division Championship. His total of fifteen goals included a hat-trick in an 8–1 home win over Shrewsbury Town.

He went on to score fifty two goals in 262 games before being transferred to West Bromwich Albion for £65,000

Ronnie Rees.

in March 1968. After just one season at the Hawthorns, he had a brief spell with Nottingham Forest before moving to Swansea City in January 1972.

REGIS, CYRILLE

Cyrille Regis was born in Maripiasoula in French Guyana. He was spotted playing non-league football for Hayes by West Bromwich Albion's then chief scout, Ronnie Allen, and after joining the Baggies, scored twice on his debut against Rotherham United. Regis scored a number of spectacular goals during the 1977–78 season and by the time Ron Atkinson had arrived at the Hawthorns to manage the Albion, he was part

Cyrille Regis.

of a great side that went close to winning the League Championship in 1979. He was the club's leading goal scorer for three successive seasons until the arrival of Garry Thompson in 1983. At the Hawthorns Regis, who had won four full England caps, scored 140 goals in almost 400 games before leaving to join Coventry City for £300,000 in October 1984.

Following his debut for the Sky Blues in a 1–1 draw at home to Newcastle United, he struggled to find his form but he did score twice in the 4–1 win over Everton on the final day of the season to help the club avoid relegation. In 1985–86 Regis equalled the club scoring record when he netted five times in the 7–2 League Cup win over Chester.

Fast, skilful and powerfully built, Regis had a super season in 1986–87, scoring sixteen goals in fifty one games and helping the Sky Blues win the FA Cup. His goal in the 3–1 sixth round win at Sheffield Wednesday was memorable as he powered through from the halfway line, leaving the Owls' defenders trailing behind him before shooting past the Wednesday 'keeper from the edge of the area. Regis went on to score sixty two goals in 282 games for Coventry before later playing for Aston Villa, Wolves, Wycombe Wanderers and Chester.

RELEGATION

Coventry City have been relegated on just two occasions. Their first taste came in 1924–25 when, after six seasons of playing Second Division football following their election to the league, they finished bottom of Division Two. It was a disastrous season for the club as it won just one away game and had a spell of twelve matches without a win, including eight successive defeats.

The club was relegated for a second time in 1951–52 when it finished the season in twenty first place in the Second Division. Between 8 September and 24 November City failed to win any of their eleven matches but three successive wins over Christmas gave them hope of avoiding the drop. In the penultimate game of the campaign they were at home to Sheffield Wednesday who needed two points to win promotion. The Owls won 2–0 to condemn the Highfield Road club to Third Division football in 1952–53.

ROBERTS, BRIAN

Manchester-born 'Harry' Roberts was christened Brian but from his early days with Coventry City he was given the nickname 'Harry' after a notorious gangster from the late 1960s.

Roberts made his debut for the Sky Blues in a 4–1 defeat at Tottenham Hotspur in April 1976 but it was 1980–81 before he established himself fully in the Coventry side. In nine seasons at Highfield Road, Roberts, who appeared in 249 League and Cup games, wore seven different numbered shirts before leaving to join Birmingham City for £10,000.

In his second season at St Andrew's he helped the club win promotion to the First Division. He stayed with the Blues for six seasons, playing in more than 200 League and Cup games before leaving to join Wolverhampton Wanderers on a free transfer.

ROBERTS, TED

Chesterfield-born forward, Ted Roberts, began his career with local side Glapwell Colliery before signing for Derby County. Unable to win a regular place in the Rams' side, he joined Coventry City in 1937 and made a goal scoring debut in a 4–0 home win over Bradford. In the years leading up to the Second World War he found himself in and out of the Coventry side and had scored twelve goals in forty four games when war broke out.

When League football resumed in 1946–47, Ted Roberts was almost thirty years old but still went on to give the Highfield Road club six years good service. He continued to score goals, his best season being 1948–49 when he netted nineteen times in thirty five outings. His last season with Coventry was 1951–52, a campaign which saw him score his only hat-trick for the club in a 3–3 home draw against Nottingham Forest.

Roberts had scored eighty seven goals in 223 League and Cup games when he left Highfield Road to play non-league football for King's Lynn.

He later returned to the club to become assistant coach and trainer/coach under Billy Frith's management but lost his job in December 1961 along with Frith, Alf Wood and Arthur Jepson.

S

SCOTT–WALFORD, FRANK

Frank Scott-Walford was an amateur goalkeeper with Tottenham Hotspur and Isthmian League club, London Caldeonians, before becoming a referee in the Southern League. Scott-Walford also helped to establish the Enfield and District League before he took up his first managerial post with Brighton and Hove Albion in March 1905. However, within two months, all but three of his playing staff had departed. However, he managed to get a team together but he was suspended for three months for illegal approaches to players. Despite the ban, Leeds directors thought he could do a job for them and brought him to Elland Road. He brought in many of his trusted Brighton players but none made a lasting impact. He later switched his attention to Ireland but with little cash to spend on new players, he found it difficult to make an impression and at the end of the 1911–12 season, Leeds had to seek re–election.

Coventry had just dropped into the Second Division of the Southern League when Scott-Walford took over there in 1914. Many of the club's matches were in South Wales and so not surrisingly it made a huge loss due to the increased travelling costs. Scott-Walford just managed to keep the club going but when business was wound up in 1915 he was still owed £100 in wages.

SECOND DIVISION

Coventry City have had three spells in the Second Division. Their first began in 1919–20 when they were admitted to the Football League and lasted for six seasons until they were relegated to the Third Division (North) in 1924–25. In fact, it took the club twenty matches before they won their first Second Division game, beating Stoke 3–2 on Christmas Day. The club's second spell in Division Two began in 1936–37, after City had won the Third Division (South) Championship the previous season. This time they spent nine seasons in the Second Division before being relegated in 1951–52.

The club's third and last spell in the Second Division began in 1964–65 after it had won the Third Division Championship in 1963–64. After finishing third in Division Two in 1965–66 the Sky Blues won the Second Division Championship the following season, finishing one point ahead of runners-up, Wolverhampton Wanderers.

SEMI-FINALS

Up to the end of the 1999–2000 season Coventry City have been involved in one FA Cup semi-final and two Football League Cup semi-finals.

SEXTON, DAVE

The son of a Southern Area middleweight boxing champion, Dave Sexton played his early football with Chelmsford City before moving on to

Luton Town. He signed for West Ham United in March 1953 and scored some valuable goals for the Hammers including a hat-trick in a 3–0 home win over Rotherham United in September 1953. While at Upton Park he played for the FA against the RAF but in the summer of 1956 he moved to Orient and from there to Brighton. He later played for Crystal Palace but a knee injury ended his career.

As a manager he helped Chelsea to the FA Cup Final of 1970 and the European Cup Winners' Cup Final of 1971. He led his next two clubs, Queen's Park Rangers and Manchester United, to the runners-up spot in the First Division as he had with Chelsea.

In May 1981 he was appointed manager of Coventry City, but in his first season in

Dave Sexton.

charge the club struggled against relegation and when it just missed the drop in 1982–83 as well Sexton was sacked. The decision was much to the disgust of his loyal players. Later that year, Sexton was appointed assistant to England manager, Bobby Robson. He also played a leading role in the newly formed soccer school of excellence.

SILLETT, JOHN

John Sillett began his Football League career with Chelsea, where he played alongside his brother, Peter, who went on to win full international honours for England. A strong, hard-tackling full-back, he had played in 102 games for Chelsea when he became one of Jimmy Hill's first signings for the Highfield Road club.

He made his debut in a 2–0 home defeat at the hands of Hull City in April 1962 and then hardly missed a game over the next two seasons which culminated in the club winning the Third Division Championship in 1963–64. During its early days in the Second Division, Sillett slipped a disc and after playing in 128 games, joined Plymouth Argyle.

On leaving Home Park he spent six years coaching Bristol City before being appointed manager of Hereford United. After taking the Edgar Street club to the Third Division Championship in 1975–76 he was brought back to Highfield Road as coach by former team mate Bobby Gould.

However, within a year he had lost his job as the Sky Blues began to struggle. Don Mackay re-employed him and in May 1986, 'Snozz' became the club's chief coach when Mackay resigned. He formed a successful managerial partnership with George Curtis and together they brought an expressive type of football to the club which resulted in Coventry winning the FA Cup in 1987, beating Spurs 3–2 in the final. Sillett was rewarded with promotion to team manager but within three years he had been relieved of his duties following FA Cup defeats at the hands of Sutton United and Northampton Town. He later returned to Edgar Street to manage Hereford United for a second time.

SIMOD CUP

The Simod Cup replaced the Full Members' Cup for the 1987–88 season. After receiving byes in the first two rounds of the competition, City faced

Wimbledon at Highfield Road and in a highly entertaining game two goals from Dave Bennett gave the Sky Blues a 2–1 win. Drawn at home in the quarter-final against Ipswich Town, the Sky Blues won 2–0 with Gynn and Phillips the goal scorers. In the semi-final City faced Reading, who were then bottom of the Second Division. A crowd of 15,348 crammed into Elm Park to see the sides play out a 1–1 draw after extra time, with David Speedie netting for Coventry. For the first time in the club's history a penalty shoot out was needed to decide which team would play in the Wembley final. Sadly, Reading triumphed 4–3 in a match that did not finish until 10.30 pm.

The Sky Blues again received byes in the first two rounds of the 1988–89 competition but then lost 1–0 at Middlesbrough in round three.

SIMPSON, NOEL

Noel Simpson played for both Nottingham clubs in war-time league matches before signing for Forest at the end of the hostilities. He spent two seasons in their first team, appearing in forty seven league games before Coventry manager, Billy Frith, paid the City Ground club £8,000 for his services in the summer of 1948.

He played his first game for the Sky Blues in a 2–2 draw at Brentford on the opening day of the 1948–49 season and was a first team regular for the next nine seasons despite suffering serious knee injuries in 1950–51 and 1953–54.

Simpson, who played the majority of his games at left-half, was a ball winner and one of only a few players to perform with any consistency in what was a period of upheaval for the club. Towards the end of his Highfield Road career he was appointed club captain but in February 1957, after playing in 270 League and Cup games, he was allowed to leave the club and join Exeter City where he ended his career after making thirty three league appearances for the Grecians.

SKOL FESTIVAL

In the summer of 1979, the Sky Blues were invited to take part in the pre=season Skol Festival tournament. All the games were played at one or other of the major grounds in Edinburgh. After beating Manchester

City 3–1 in their opening match, Coventry then defeated Hearts by the same scoreline and so when they met Hibernian at Easter Road, needed only a draw to win the trophy. With goalkeeper Jim Blyth in superb form, they played out a goal-less draw and so won the trophy.

SKY BLUE SONG

The Sky Blue Song, which is sung to the tune of the *Eton Boating Song*, was written by the schoolmaster and poet, William Johnson Cory, in 1865.

> Let's all sing together,
> Play up Sky Blues,
> While we sing together,
> We will never lose,
> Tottenham or Chelsea,
> United or anyone,
> They can't defeat us,
> We'll fight 'til the game is won.

SMALLEST PLAYER

Although such statistics are always unreliable for those playing around the turn of the century, the distinction of being Coventry City's smallest player must go to Micky Gynn. He was 5ft 3ins.

SMITH, BILLY

Billy Smith played his early football for West Bromwich Baptists, where his goal scoring feats included scoring six goals in a match against Handsworth. Not surprisingly his prolific marksmanship attracted the attention of the bigger clubs and after a spell with Worcester City, he went to West Bromwich Albion in 1902.

He joined Coventry City in the summer of 1907 and the following season topped the club's scoring charts in the Birmingham League with thirty three goals in thirty three games. He scored five in the 11–2 win over West Bromwich Albion Reserves; four in the 6–0 home defeat of Brierley Hill; and hat-tricks against Stourbridge (Away 9–1) and Stoke Reserves (Home 5–0). At the end of the season the club failed to re-sign him and he joined Small Heath. He returned to Highfield Road for the start of the 1909–10 season and although he continued to find the net, he also turned provider with many of his pinpoint crosses being converted by his team mates.

At the end of the 1911–12 season, Smith left Highfield Road for a second time but returned for one more season in 1913. Sadly he failed to recapture his old form and, having scored sixty four goals in 130 games in his three spells with the club, hung up his boots.

SOUTHERN LEAGUE

City were elected to the Southern League in 1908 and drew their first match 1–1 with Crystal Palace. Following four successive defeats they found themselves at the foot of the league. They continued to struggle and ended the season in twentieth place. The Southern League committee decided to increase the league to twenty two members and so City did not have to apply for re–election.

In 1909–10 the club's successful FA Cup run led to a loss of league form and it finished eighth after being near the top of the table for most of the season.

Coventry's best finish in the Southern League was 1911–12 when they finished sixth, recording their biggest win in Division One, 9–0 against Brentford. However, two seasons later, City were relegated after finishing bottom of the league and in 1914–15, their last season of Southern League football, they finished fifth. During the course of the season they beat Newport County 10–1.

SOUTHERN PROFESSIONAL FLOODLIGHT CUP

This competition, which ran for five seasons, began in 1955–56 but Coventry did not enter until 1958–59 when they were knocked out in the first round following a 6–1 defeat at Millwall. In 1959–60 City beat Southend United 4–0, following a goal-less draw at Roots Hall, and Fulham 1–0, after the first match had been drawn 1–1, to win a place in the semi-final. Two goals from Ray Straw helped Coventry beat Southampton and so face West Ham United in the final. A crowd of 16,921 were at Highfield Road to see Ron Hewitt score both the club's goals in a 2–1 win over the Hammers. As this was the last season the competition was held, Coventry City were the last holders of the cup.

SPEEDIE, DAVID

Striker David Speedie began his career with Barnsley but after being unable to hold down a regular first team place, left to play for Darlington. After netting seventeen goals for the Quakers in 1981–82 he joined Chelsea and in five seasons with the Stamford Bridge club scored forty seven goals in 162 league games. His form during this period also led to him winning the first of ten caps for Scotland when he played against England in 1985.

David Speedie.

In July 1987 Coventry paid a club record fee of £780,000 to bring Speedie to Highfield Road. He made his debut in the opening match of the 1987–88 season, scoring one of the goals in a 2–1 win over Spurs. Speedie became a great favourite with the Coventry faithful and in 1988–89, when City finished seventh in Division One, he was the leading scorer with fourteen goals in thirty six, games including a hat-trick in a 4–3 home defeat by Middlesbrough.

He had scored thirty five goals in 144 first team outings when he was sold to Liverpool for £700,000. He spent just six months at Anfield before joining Blackburn Rovers where he scored twenty three goals in thirty six games. He then moved to Southampton where he had loan spells with Birmingham City, West Bromwich Albion and West Ham United before joining Leicester City where he ended his league career.

SPONSORS

The club's present sponsors are Subaru. Previous sponsors include Peugeot, Glazepta, Granada Bingo and Talbot.

STANLEY, WILLIAM

William Stanley was the founder of Coventry City Football Club and also its first secretary. In that capacity he arranged all the club's fixture lists and was successful in applying for membership of the Warwickshire Football Association. Stanley also played at centre-forward for the club but in 1885, after two years' association with Singers, he was replaced by centre-half and vice-captain, Harry Hathaway.

STEIN, COLIN

Colin Stein joined Glasgow Rangers from Hibernian and in his time at

Ibrox Park he won seventeen Scottish caps and helped the club win the European Cup Winners' Cup. In October 1972 he was surprisingly allowed to join Coventry City for £100,000 – with winger Quinton Young included in the deal. He made his Sky Blues' debut in a 1–0 win at Crystal Palace and ended the season with twelve goals in thirty five games. In 1973–74 his form was such that he added another four Scottish caps to his collection. Although he found goals harder to come by he did net a hat-trick in a 5–1 second round League Cup win over Darlington.

Stein, who was extremely popular with the Highfield Road fans, had scored twenty nine goals in ninety eight games for City when manager Gordon Milne sold him back to Rangers for £80,000 in 1975.

Sadly his return to Ibrox coincided with a loss of form and three years later he hung up his boots.

STORER, HARRY

The son of a famous England and Liverpool goalkeeper and nephew of a Derbyshire and England cricketer, he had trials with Notts County and Millwall before turning professional with Grimsby Town. At Blundell Park he developed into a tough tackling wing-half and in 1921 moved to Derby County for £4,500. During the 1923–24 season he played at inside-forward and after scoring twenty seven goals in forty two games was rewarded with the first of two full caps for England.

In February 1929 he moved to Burnley for a large fee after scoring forty three goals in 274 games for the Rams. After two years at Turf Moor he became manager of Coventry City. After signing Clarrie Bourton from Bristol City the club was soon heading for promotion. It finished second in 1933–34; third in 1934–35; and won the Third Division Championship in 1935–36. Storer, surprisingly, left Highfield Road in 1945 to take charge of Birmingham City, probably in the belief that he had achieved all he could at Coventry.

In his first season at St Andrew's he led the Blues to the semi-finals of the FA Cup, where they lost after a replay to his former club Derby County, and to the Football League (South) Championship. In 1947–48 he took Birmingham to the Second Division Championship but by November 1948 he was back at Highfield Road.

He remained with Coventry until December 1953 and, after a spell out of management, took over the reins at Derby County and succeeded in taking them into the Second Division. He stayed in charge until his retirement in 1962, later scouting for the club until his death five years later.

STRACHAN, GORDON

Gordon Strachan began his illustrious career with Dundee but after sixty appearances for the Dens Park club he moved to Aberdeen for a fee of £50,000 in November 1977. While at Pittodrie he won just about every honour possible – two Premier Division Championship medals in 1979–80 and 1983–84; three Scottish Cup winners' medals between 1982 and 1984; and a European Cup winners' medal in 1983. His form was such that at the end of that first successful season he won the first of fifty full caps for

Gordon Strachan.

Scotland and in May 1980 he was selected to play against Northern Ireland. Having scored eighty nine goals in 298 games for Aberdeen he joined Manchester United in the summer of 1984.

By the end of his first season with the Old Trafford club he had won an FA Cup winners' medal, following the 1–0 extra time win over Everton. In almost five years with United he had been an automatic choice so it was a great surprise when he left to join Leeds United in March 1989.

Appointed captain for the coming season he led Leeds, by example, to the Second Division Championship as an ever-present and top scorer with sixteen goals. In 1991 he was named Footballer of the Year and in 1991–92 helped Leeds win the League Championship. He went on to score forty five goals in 245 games for the Elland Road club before joining Coventry City as assistant manager in March 1995.

He made his debut for the club in a 2–0 home win over Sheffield Wednesday the following month, going on to appear in thirty three games over the next three seasons, when his services were needed. In November 1996 he became the club's manager and although Coventry won their last five games before the turn of the year they ended the season in seventeenth place. In 1997–98 Strachan led the Sky Blues to eleventh place, their joint highest Premiership position and their second highest Premiership points total. In 1998–99 they finished in fifteenth place, six points above the relegation zone.

STRAW, RAY

Centre-forward Ray Straw began his career with his home team, Ilkeston Town, while working down the pit before signing for Derby County in October 1951. However, it was 1955–56 before he won a regular place in the Rams' side and the following season he equalled the club's scoring record with thirty seven goals in forty four games as it won the Third Division (North) Championship. He had scored fifty seven goals in ninety four league games for Derby when Billy Frith brought him to Highfield Road in November 1957.

He made his debut in a 4–1 home defeat by Millwall and he went on to score fourteen goals in twenty two games. City still finished nineteenth and had to play the 1958–59 season in the newly formed Division Four. That season Straw was the club's top scorer with twenty seven goals as City finished runners-up to Port Vale and won immediate promotion. His total included a hat-trick in the 7–1 home win over Aldershot. Straw topped the club's scoring charts again in 1959–60, netting twenty goals in forty three games as City finished fourth in Division Three. Straw, who created history in the opening game against Mansfield Town by becoming the first player to have appeared in all six divisions of the Football League, secured a hat-trick in the return game as the Stags were beaten 4–2 at Field Mill.

At the end of the following season Straw, who had scored eighty five goals in 151 games, was rather surprisingly allowed to join Mansfield Town. He helped them win promotion to the Third Division in 1962–63 before leaving to play non-league football for Lockheed-Leamington.

SUBSTITUTES

Coventry City's first substitute was Dietmar Bruck who came on for Ron Farmer in the club's fifth game of the 1965–66 season, a 3–3 draw against Manchester City at Highfield Road. The club's first goal scoring Number 12 was Bobby Gould who scored in City's 3–3 draw at Nottingham Forest on 22 August 1967.

The greatest number of substitutes used in a single season by the Sky Blues under the single substitute rule was thirty five in 1983–84. From 1986–87 two substitutes were allowed and in 1991–92 the club used fifty six. In recent seasons three substitutes have been allowed and in 1996–97 City used sixty. The greatest number of substitute appearances for the Sky Blues has been made by Peter Ndlovu who came on during thirty six league games and another four in the FA Cup, including an extraordinary fourteen league appearances in the substitute's shirt during the season of 1991–92.

SUNDAY FOOTBALL

On 30 December 1970 Coventry City applied to the Football League for permission to play four experimental league games in March 1971 on Sundays. The request was turned down.

The first Sunday matches in the Football League took place on 20 January 1974 during the three-day week imposed by the government during its trial of strength with the coalminers. Coventry City had to wait until the following Sunday, 27 January, before playing their first game on the Sabbath, drawing 0–0 at home to Derby County in a fourth round FA Cup game watched by a crowd of 41,281.

SUSTAINED SCORING

During the 1931–32 season, when Coventry finished twelfth in the Third Division (South), Clarrie Bourton proved himself to be a prolific goal scorer. His first two goals came in the third game as City beat Thames 2–0. He later scored in eleven consecutive games, netting five in the 6–1 home win over Bournemouth and a hat-trick in the 4–2 defeat of Clapton Orient. He later scored four against Mansfield Town (Home 5–1) and hat-tricks against Reading (Home 5–1), Crystal Palace (Home 8–0), Mansfield Town (Away 3–3) and Watford (Home 5–0). Bourton ended the season with forty nine goals in forty league games.

T

TALLEST PLAYER

It is impossible to say for certain who has been the tallest player ever on Coventry's books as such records are notoriously unreliable. But almost certain to lay claim to the distinction is Steve Ogrizovic, who stands 6ft 4ins.

TELEVISION SCREEN

In October 1965 the club relayed live action from its match at Cardiff City on to a huge screen at Highfield Road – the first club to do so. A crowd of 10,295 watched as the Sky Blues won 2–1 with goals by Rees and Curtis. It was billed as the first game ever to be staged in two separate grounds. A crowd of 12,639 watched the game at Ninian Park.

TEXACO CUP

The predecessor of the Anglo-Scottish Cup, it was launched in 1970–71 and was for English, Irish and Scottish club sides not involved in European competition. Coventry first entered in 1971–72 and despite losing 1–0 at Falkirk in their first round first leg match, won 3–0 in the return at Highfield Road to progress into the second round. A Jeff Blockley goal gave City a 1–1 draw at home to Newcastle United but despite the centre-half netting again at St James Park, the Magpies won 5–1 to take the tie 6–2 on aggregate.

In 1972–73 Coventry were held to a 3–3 draw at home by Motherwell with Billy Rafferty scoring two of the club's goals. In the second leg at Fir Park, Motherwell scored the only goal of the game to put the Sky Blues out of the competition at the first hurdle.

The following season City again faced Motherwell in the opening round of the competition but this time lost both matches 1–0 at home and 3–2 at Fir Park.

THIRD DIVISION

Coventry City have had three spells in the Third Division. Following their relegation from Division Two in 1924–25 they played a season in the Third Division (North). At the end of that campaign Stoke and Stockport County were relegated from Division Two and that enabled Coventry to switch to the Third Division (South). The move did little to improve results but it did help the club financially from a travelling point of view. City spent a further ten seasons in the Third Division (South) before winning the Championship and promotion in 1935–36 after two seasons of coming close to clinching the title.

The club's second spell of Third Division football began in 1952–53 following its relegation from Division Two. That season saw City finish in sixth place and that was to be their best performance in this spell for in 1957–58 they nineteenth in the Third Division (South) and, following reorganisation, found themselves in Division Four for the season of 1958–59.

City won promotion at the first attempt and began their third and final spell in Division Three in 1959–60. The club came close to winning promotion that season, finishing fourth, a position they also finished in 1962–63. However, in 1963–64 City won the Third Division Championship and returned to Division Two after a break of twelve years.

THOMAS, DANNY

As a schoolboy Danny Thomas had trials with both Leeds United and Sheffield United before deciding to join Coventry City, where he developed into a potential England regular. After playing in a League Cup defeat at West Bromwich Albion he made his league debut as a substitute in a 1–1 draw at home to Spurs in September 1979.

He soon established himself in a talented young Coventry team, winning his first England Under-21 cap against the Republic of Ireland in March 1981. He collected four more caps at that level and played twice for the full England team on the tour to Australia in 1983 before moving to Spurs for £250,000 in June 1983.

Thomas, who had scored six goals in 130 games for Coventry, spent most of his first season at White Hart Lane on the treatment table, although he did play in both legs of the 1984 UEFA Cup Final and won two more Under-21 caps against Italy and Spain in May 1984.

An exciting full-back able to play on either flank, he had just got back to his very best form and was being tipped to gain further international honours when he suffered a terrible knee injury against Queen's Park Rangers in March 1987. It not only forced him to miss the FA Cup Final against his former club but brought his career to a premature end. He retired from playing in January 1988 and went to study for a new career in physiotherapy, eventually returning to the game as Ossie Ardilles' physio at West Bromwich Albion.

THOMPSON, GARRY

Birmingham-born Garry Thompson, whose brother Keith also played for the Sky Blues, made his Coventry debut in a 3–2 home defeat by Aston Villa in March 1978. Over the next three seasons he scored seventeen goals in forty six games before establishing himself as a first team regular in 1980–81 when he was the club's top scorer with fifteen goals. Included in that total were six goals in the club's run to the League Cup semi-finals. He continued to find the net for the Sky Blues over the next two seasons but in February 1983 this England Under-21 international joined West Bromwich Albion for £225,000.

Thompson, who had scored forty nine goals in 158 games for Coventry, teamed up with Cyrille Regis at the Hawthorns but after just one season, Regis left to join the Sky Blues. Thompson went on to score thirty nine goals in ninety one games for the Baggies before signing for Sheffield Wednesday for what was a club record fee of £450,000.

He failed to adapt his style of play to fit in with Wednesday's pattern and, although he scored in four consecutive games around the turn of the year, he left the club after one season to join Aston Villa. He later played for Watford, Crystal Palace, Queen's Park Rangers, Cardiff City and Northampton Town.

TICKLE, CHARLIE

Charlie Tickle began his Football League career with Small Heath where, in six seasons with the Birmingham club, he scored fourteen goals in ninety games. His performances had led to him winning a Junior international cap against Scotland and representing the Football League. He joined Coventry City in the summer of 1908 and played his first game for the club on the opening day of the 1908–09 Southern League season in a 1–1 draw against Crystal Palace. Tickle was a virtual ever-present in his three seasons with the club and was appointed captain shortly after his arrival at Highfield Road. His accurate crosses from the right-wing provided many goal scoring opportunities for both Harry Buckle and Charlie Warren but in 1910–11 he too proved he could score goals, netting ten in thirty five games to be the club's second top scorer.

He had scored twenty goals in 125 Southern League and FA Cup games when in the summer of 1911 he left the club to play for Bournbrook.

TOURS

On 6 April 1932, Coventry City made their first trip abroad, playing a Dutch XI at Sparta's ground in Rotterdam. Coventry won 3–0 with goals from Cull, Lauderdale and Bourton.

The club's first tour came at the end of the 1946–47 season when they won three and drew one of their four matches in Denmark.

Coventry's biggest win on tour came against the Bermuda Police in Hamilton when they completed their visit to the West Indies with an 8–0 win. On 13 June 1972, City played Brazilian side Santos and drew 2–2 with a certain Pele scoring one of the goals for the South American club.

TRANSFERS

The club's record transfer fee received is £13 million that Inter Milan paid for Republic of Ireland international Robbie Keane in July 2000. City's record transfer fee paid out is £6 million for the same player to Wolverhampton Wanderers twelve months earlier.

U

UNDEFEATED

The club's best and longest undefeated home squence in the Football League is of nineteen matches between 11 April 1925 and 13 March 1926. Coventry's longest run of undefeated Football League matches home and away is twenty five between 26 November 1966 and 13 May 1967.

UNUSUAL GOALS

One of the cheekiest and most unusual goals was scored by City's Ernie Hunt in the 3–1 defeat of Everton on 3 October 1970. Willie Carr jumped with the ball between his legs to set up Hunt's volley from a free kick. Seen by millions on *Match of the Day* it became known as the 'donkey kick'.

In the FA Cup match against Northampton Town on 20 November 1954 Roy Kirk hit a long upfield pass, but the ball bounced over goalkeeper Alf Wood's head and into the net from 80 yards.

V

VICTORIES IN A SEASON – HIGHEST

In seasons 1935–36 and 1958–59 Coventry City won twenty four of their forty two and forty six league matches respectively as they won the Third Division (South) Championship in the former season, and were runners-up in the Fourth Division in the latter.

VICTORIES IN A SEASON – LOWEST

Coventry's poorest performance was in 1995–96 when they won only eight matches out of their thirty eight league games and finished sixteenth in the Premier League.

WALLACE, IAN

Ian Wallace began his career with Dumbarton before joining Coventry City for a fee of £40,000 in the summer of 1976. He made his debut for

the Sky Blues as a substitute in a 2–1 home defeat by Sunderland in October 1976, ending the season with nine goals in twenty six games, including a hat-trick in a 5–2 win over Stoke City. Yet just before Christmas in Wallace's first season with the club he was hurled through the windscreen of a car in a road accident and forced to miss two months of the season.

In 1977–78 he formed a prolific goal scoring partnership with Mick Ferguson and was the club's leading scorer with twenty one goals in forty one league games, including six in the opening four games of the season. His performances this season led to him winning the first of three full caps for Scotland when he scored in the match against Bulgaria. Wallace had scored sixty goals in 140 League and Cup games for Coventry when in July 1980 he joined Nottingham Forest for a club record £1.25 million.

He scored thirty six goals in 134 lweague games for Forest before joining Brest. He

Ian Wallace.

returned to these shores in January 1985 to see out his league career with Sunderland. He later had a spell with CS Martino of Madeira before moving to play in Australia.

WARNER, LESLIE

Nicknamed 'Plum' after the Middlesex and England cricketer Sir Pelham Warner, he made a sensational debut against Swansea in February 1938, having a hand in all Coventry's goals in a 5–0 win. Despite his performance in that game, Warner only played in a handful of games for City before the outbreak of the Second World War. During the hostilities he served in Northern Ireland with the Royal Warwickshire Regiment.

Warner returned to Highfield Road towards the end of 1945 but found that he had competition for the number seven shirt from Dennis Simpson and it was not until 1948–49 that he won a regular place in the side. His best season for the club was 1950–51 when Coventry finished seventh in Division Two. During that campaign he and Norman Lockhart provided a series of pinpoint crosses on which Ken Chisholm and Ted Roberts thrived.

He played the last of his 207 games in which he scored twenty two goals, against Brighton in January 1954, almost eighteen years after first joining the club.

WARREN, HARRY

The son of Ben Warren who won twenty two caps for England, he played his football for Exeter City, Sheffield United and Merthyr Town but was never as good as his father. After a spell as player/manager of Folkestone, he managed both Chelmsford and Southend United during the war as they played at the same ground. He managed Southend United for sixteen years with 1955–56 being his best season as the Shrimpers finished fourth in the Southern Section.

In June 1956 he left Roots Hall to become manager of Coventry City. The team made a good start to the 1956–57 season but a rift soon developed between him and the players over wages. Morale sagged as a number of the Coventry side saw Warren as being too soft. He was given very little money to spend on new players and the club slipped down the league to end the season in sixteenth place. After a poor start to the 1957–58 season Warren was sacked, no doubt regretting his decision to leave Southend.

WARTIME FOOTBALL

In spite of the outbreak of war in 1914 the football leagues embarked upon their planned programme of matches for the ensuing season and these were completed on schedule at the end of April the following year. The season saw Coventry finish fifth in the Southern League Division Two. It was then decided to abandon both the FA Cup and Southern League competitions and to cancel the professional players' contracts. A number of charity matches were played at the ground but it was not until 1918-19 before any organised football took place. That season City finished ninth in the English League Midland Section.

In contrast to the events of 1914, once war was declared on 3 September 1939 the Football League programme of 1939-40 was immediately suspended. The government forbade any major sporting events, so that for a while there was no football of any description. At the start of the 1939-40 season City won one and drew two of the three matches played and were in third place in the Second Division when the competition was aborted. When football resumed City entered the Regional League Midland Division and finished third. The highlight of the 1939-40 season being a 10-2 win over Luton Town. The club finished third in the South Regional League in 1940-41 before spending the next three wartime seasons in the Football League North Championship and a best position of seventh in 1941-42. In 1945-46, City finished thirteenth in the Football League South.

WHELAN, NOEL

A one-time ball boy at Elland Road, Noel Whelan joined his home team after leaving school and turned professional in March 1993. An England Youth international, he was a member of the squad which won the European Youth Championship in 1993 and the Leeds side which won the FA Youth Cup in the same year, scoring one of the goals in the first leg of the final at Old Trafford. He made good progress and scored on his debut for England Under-21s against the Republic of Ireland. He had scored eight goals in fifty five games for Leeds when Coventry paid £2 million for his services in December 1995.

After making his Sky Blues debut in a 4-1 defeat at Aston Villa, he scored seven goals in his first eleven games for the club as it finished sixteenth the Premier League. Following an indifferent season in 1996–97 Whelan matured into a fine all-rounder, playing in a much deeper role behind Darren Huckerby and Dion Dublin, although in 1998–99 he reverted to his role as striker. Voted the Supporters' Player of the Year in 1999 Whelan, scored thirty five goals in 151 games for the Highfield Road club before joining Middlesborough for £2.2 million.

WOOD, ALF

Goalkeeper Alf Wood played for Sutton Town and Nuneaton Borough before joining Coventry City in December 1935. He made his debut in a 5–0 home win over Swansea Town in February 1938 but only made one more league appearance before the outbreak of the Second World War.

During the war, Wood played for the army and guested for Northampton Town but he contracted spinal meningitis and was told he would never play again. Happily he recovered and, after playing at Burnley on the opening day league football resumed in August 1946, he went on to play in 209 consecutive league games. In September 1951 he lost is place to Peter Taylor and decided to join Northampton Town on a permanent basis. He appeared in 139 games for the Cobblers before returning to Highfield Road as the club's assistant trainer. However, he went on to play in a number of games, making his last appearance at the age of 44 years 207 days against Plymouth Argyle in December 1958. Wood, who had played in 246 League and Cup games for City, continued as the club's trainer before losing his job after City had been beaten 2–1 by King's Lynn in the FA Cup competition of 1961–62.

He later managed Walsall, where he 'discovered' Allan Clarke, but stayed only one season at Fellows Park. He returned to Coventry to run the works side at Massey Ferguson, a team which included many former professionals.

WORST START

The club's worst start to a season was in 1919–20, its inaugural season in the Football League. It played twenty league games before its first victory of the season, drawing five and losing fourteen of the opening fixtures. The dismal run ended with a 3–2 home win over Stoke on Christmas Day 1919.

'X'

In football 'x' traditionally stands for a draw. The club record for the number of draws in season was in 1962–63 when it drew seventeen matches.

XMAS DAY

There was a time when football matches were regularly played on Christmas Day but in recent years the game's authorities have dropped the fixture from the calendar.

Coventry played their first game on Christmas Day in 1902 when they were members of the Birmingham and District League, losing 1–0 against Small Heath Reserves. In the club's first season of League Football Christmas Day 1919 was a double celebration for Coventry City. Not only did they beat Stoke 3–2 but also the three goals scored were the first the side had been able to achieve in Division Two for nearly three months.

When Coventry beat Wolves 7–1 on Christmas Day 1924 Toms scored a hat-trick, a feat that was repeated in 1931 as Clarrie Bourton netted a hat-trick in a 5–1 home win over Reading. Quite remarkably, the first fourteen of Coventry's fixtures on Christmas Day were played at Highfield Road and it was 1937 before City had to travel. When they did so, they lost 3–2 at Sheffield United.

The last time Coventry City played a Football League game on Christmas Day was in 1959 when a crowd of 17,468 saw City beat Wrexham 5–3 at Highfield Road, with Ken Satchwell scoring four of the goals.

Y

YORATH, TERRY

An often under valued member of the great Leeds United side of the late 1960s and early 1970s, the rugged blond Welsh international won fifty nine caps. He left Elland Road in the summer of 1976, joining Coventry for a fee of £125,000. He made his debut for the Sky Blues in a 3–1 defeat at Liverpool in the fourth game of the 1976–77 season and went on to play in all but one game in that campaign, with his first goal for the club being the winner against Birmingham City. In 1977–78, Yorath was outstanding as City finished seventh in the First Division, his perform-ances alongside Barry Powell in the Coventry midfield being the major reason for the club's upturn in fortune. Sadly the following season saw him hampered by injury and at the end of that 1978–79 campaign after which he had scored three goals in 107 games, he joined Tottenham Hotspur for £275,000.

At White Hart Lane he showed that he possessed a shrewd grasp of tactics and was an accomplished distributor of ther ball but injuries again restricted his appearances and in the summer of 1981 he moved to play for Vancouver Whitecaps.

He later returned to this country to launch a successful career in coach-ing and management, taking charge of both Bradford City and Swansea before becoming the national manager of Wales.

YOUNGEST PLAYER

The youngest player to appear in a first–class fixture for Coventry City is Brian Hill who played in the Third Division (South) match against Gillingham at the Priestfield Stadium on 30 April 1958 when he was 16 years 281 days old. In fact, he scored the club's first goal in a 3–2 defeat.

YOUTH CUP

Coventry City have reached the FA Youth Cup Final on four occasions, winning the trophy in 1987.

In 1967–68, the Sky Blues met Burnley in the two-legged final, winning the first leg at Highfield Road 2–1 with goals from Paddon and Allen, and losing 2–0 at Turf Moor in the return leg.

Two seasons later, City reached the final again where they met Tottenham Hotspur. Both teams won their home leg 1–0 with Jimmy Holmes scoring from the penalty spot at Highfield Road. The Sky Blues won the toss for he right to hold the replay but in front of a Highfield Road crowd of 14,926, they were held to a 2–2 draw. The fourth meeting at White Hart Lane saw Spurs, with Steve Perryman and Graeme Souness in their side, triumph 1–0.

The Sky Blues eventually won the trophy in 1986–87 beating Charlton Athletic 1–0 after extra time in the second leg at Highfield Road after the first match at the Valley had ended 1–1. Steve Livingstone was the scorer of the all-important goal.

In 1998–99 Coventry reached the final again but lost 9–0 on aggregate to West Ham United.

Z

ZENITH

Few fans will argue over which moment has been the greatest in the club's 116 year history. On 16 May 1987 a Wembley crowd of 98,000 saw the Sky Blues beat Tottenham Hotspur 3–2 after extra time to win the FA Cup.

ZENITH DATA SYSTEMS CUP

The Zenith Data Systems Cup replaced the Simod Cup from the 1989–90 season. In their first match in the competition Coventry lost 3–1 at home to Wimbledon after extra time. In 1990–91 City went out at the first hurdle again, this time losing 1–0 at Derby County. The Sky Blues last appearance in the competition the following season saw them lose 2–0 at home to Aston Villa and so fail to win a match in any of their three seasons in the Zenith Data Systems Cup.